Understanding Your Schizophreni

Understanding Your Schizophrenia Illness

A Workbook

By Chris Healy

BICENTENNIAL
1807
WILEY
2007
BICENTENNIAL

John Wiley & Sons, Ltd

Other Wiley Editorial Offices

John Wiley & Sons Inc., 111 River Street, Hoboken, NJ 07030, USA

Jossey-Bass, 989 Market Street, San Francisco, CA 94103-1741, USA

Wiley-VCH Verlag GmbH, Boschstr. 12, D-69469 Weinheim, Germany

John Wiley & Sons Australia Ltd, 42 McDougall Street, Milton, Queensland 4064, Australia

John Wiley & Sons (Asia) Pte Ltd, 2 Clementi Loop #02-01, Jin Xing Distripark, Singapore 129809

John Wiley & Sons Canada Ltd, 6045 Freemont Blvd, Mississauga, ONT, L5R 4J3, Canada

Wiley also publishes its books in a variety of electronic formats. Some content that appears in print
may not be available in electronic books.

Anniversary Logo Design: Richard J. Pacifico

ISBN 978-0-470-51174-9

Typeset in 10/13pt Scala and Scala Sans by Thomson Digital, India
Printed and bound in Great Britain by Antony Rowe, Chippenham, Wiltshire
This book is printed on acid-free paper responsibly manufactured from sustainable forestry in which
at least two trees are planted for each one used for paper production

Contents

About the Author

I first trained as a general nurse over 30 years ago and admit to feeling out of my depth at times regarding understanding those with mental health issues. My ignorance and attitude were partly shaped by negative media reports. But since training as a staff nurse in psychiatry I have gained much insight and understanding of sufferers and their families.

I have worked for nearly 12 years on a medium-secure ward; most of the clients I nurse have committed crimes while suffering from their illness. It is not common that those with mental health issues commit crimes but, if their illness is left untreated and allowed to become more and more severe, sufferers who are acutely ill may unintentionally end up in prison.

Preface

Sufferers approach mental health workers asking for information regarding their illness and psychiatrists ask mental health workers to teach clients about their illness. But how does a mental health worker achieve this?

There is much information on the Internet, in books and leaflets, but it takes time to bring together and organise this information. Most mental health staff will admit to struggling with collating up-to-date information and structuring sessions for their clients.

They may have printed off some information from the Internet, educated clients from their experience of nursing those with schizophrenia or read academic literature on the subject and summarised their findings. As a result, most clients receive different levels of education regarding the understanding of their illness.

This was the problem that I encountered during my nursing career, when I was in need of a format regarding basic information for my clients, and also a framework to provide structured sessions which would aid me in educating those who suffered from schizophrenia.

So a few years ago I put together an 'understanding your schizophrenia' folder, which helped my colleagues and me to structure sessions on educating our clients about their illness. Last year, I updated the folder and decided it would be more beneficial for clients if I put it together as a workbook.

There is much information around regarding understanding schizophrenia, but I feel my workbook is unique because it allows sufferers to play a part in understanding and having an awareness of their schizophrenia by writing down their thoughts and feelings.

Also I want to communicate that if someone suffers from schizophrenia they need to learn all they can about it so that they can control their illness and not let it control them. Further, I intend to highlight that sufferers can have a successful life if they choose to and can afford to be more optimistic in their attitude towards their illness.

There are many myths surrounding schizophrenia, and some of these may be believed by sufferers, which may cause them alarm when they are diagnosed with the condition. And so another aim of this workbook is to allay those fears by exploding these misleading, popular myths.

Schizophrenia causes much emotional pain, and sufferers need to have information at the time of their distress so that they develop a belief that their problems can be identified and worked through.

The sufferer needs to proceed through the workbook with someone who has an understanding of mental illness so that support can be given when any difficult subject areas are explored. An open discussion on challenging issues that may have been previously hard to approach by health professionals without compromising their relationship is to be encouraged. It is hoped that this workbook will help families of sufferers to understand more about their relative's illness by providing many clinical and therapeutic facts about the condition. In this way, the workbook might also prove to be an accessible introduction to schizophrenia for mental health students. As it is designed to be a general introduction to schizophrenia, this workbook is intended to be useful to sufferers whether they are in-patients or receiving community-based care.

The workbook is divided into six sessions dealing with various aspects of schizophrenia. Each session begins with a questionnaire, to be completed by the sufferer. This is not a test but should be seen as a means by which the sufferer and their carer or family can share information. It will also allow the sufferer to focus upon certain aspects of their illness before each session. The sessions need to be completed at a slow pace, perhaps only a few pages a week, and it would possibly take a few months to complete the workbook. It's important that the sufferer works at their own pace to ensure that they thoroughly understand each session.

I would suggest that the workbook remain in the possession of a mental health profession-al or the sufferer's keyworker until the sessions are completely finished. This would prevent the sufferer from working through issues alone in case they might need some support. When completed, the sufferer can then keep the workbook and use it as a reference. It would also be a good idea if the literature referenced in the workbook were available for suf-ferers if they were unable to access the Internet.

The workbook could possibly be seen as a good assessment tool for health professionals, and it also would be beneficial to detained sufferers as it could be used as evidence that the suf-ferer has undertaken some work on understanding their illness when applying for a mental health tribunal or manager's hearing.

It is our responsibility as health workers to provide information for our clients that enhances their lives and offers them some hope for the future. To this end, this workbook attempts to provide a structure for the sufferer to approach, learn about and deal with their illness.

Acknowledgements

I would like to first pay special tribute to my wonderful partner Oz. Without his support and encouragement, I would not have completed this workbook.

I also would like to thank our fine outstanding sons for their patience in their attempts to help me regarding my computer literacy and for proofreading my work for any grammatical errors.

I would also like to express my thanks to Dr Kishore Seewoonarain (Consultant Forensic Psychiatrist) for his encouraging comments and his time for reading through my workbook.

I am very grateful to Rikita Patel (Senior Mental Health Pharmacist) for her informative guidance.

Finally, I would also like to thank my work colleagues for their support, but, above all, it's imperative that I mention my courageous clients, who have given me much insight into their difficult world.

Introduction

'Schizophrenia' is the name mental health professionals use to describe what they see as a form of mental illness. To suffer from schizophrenia can be a frightening experience and it can disrupt your whole life.

Schizophrenia can:

- affect your self-confidence
- cause problems with the relationship between you and your family and friends
- affect your ability to work or study
- cause some sufferers to feel like harming themselves
- cause some sufferers to commit offences when they are unwell.

This workbook is divided into sessions that will give the reader some information about their illness.

The sessions will try to explain:

- what has happened to them
- how schizophrenia affects their life
- how they can live with the illness.

These sessions aim to give you the confidence to help yourself and for you to gain some control over your illness.

It has been said that the symptoms of schizophrenia appear to be less of a problem if the sufferer, their families and professionals work together as a team. These sessions are intended to promote this relationship.

▶Understanding your illness

Below are common questions that you, your family and others ask when discussing the most common serious mental illness, schizophrenia. These questions will provide the format for the sessions and hopefully provide you with information that enhances your understanding so that you can lead a more positive life.

Session 1
What is psychosis?
What have people said about schizophrenia?
How many people in the UK suffer from schizophrenia?
Can you be tested for schizophrenia?
What is it like to suffer from schizophrenia?

Session 2
Can your parents give you schizophrenia?
Does stress cause schizophrenia?
Do illegal drugs cause schizophrenia?

Session 3
Is schizophrenia something to do with the brain?
What does *not* cause schizophrenia?
Do famous people suffer from schizophrenia?

Session 4
What are the symptoms?

Session 5
Can schizophrenia be treated?
How does medication help?
What are the side effects of my medication?
What happens if I stop taking my medication?
What will happen if I use alcohol or illegal drugs while on medication?
Can I smoke tobacco or drink caffeine?
What might happen if I experience any disturbing psychotic symptoms?
Why is it so important to keep taking my medication?

Session 6
What can I do to keep myself well?
What are the early-warning signs of a relapse in my illness?
How do I prevent a relapse?
How can I cope with my 'voices'?
What can I do to deal with my strange ideas?
How can I improve my confidence and rebuild my life?
What effect will my illness have on my relationships with my family and friends?

Session 1

These questions are not meant to be seen as a test. They are only a means of sharing information and getting you to think about your illness before you start your session. If you're not sure, just make a guess: there are no right or wrong answers.

1. How many people do you think suffer from schizophrenia in the UK?

2. What do you think the word 'psychosis' means?

3. What age were you when you first developed your illness?

4. Did you find it easy or difficult to tell the doctor about your symptoms?

5. What do you think the general public's understanding is of schizophrenia?

Session 1

During this session, we will be looking at the following frequently asked questions regarding schizophrenia.

1. What is psychosis?

2. What have people said about schizophrenia?

3. How many people in the UK suffer from schizophrenia?

4. Can you be tested for schizophrenia?

5. What is it like to suffer from schizophrenia?

Session 1

▶ WHAT IS PSYCHOSIS?

Psychiatrists divide mental illnesses into two main groups:

> **NEUROSIS** and **PSYCHOSIS**

'Neurosis' is defined as a 'a mild mental illness involving symptoms of stress (e.g. depression, anxiety, obsessive behaviour) without loss of contact with reality, and not caused by organic disease' (Pearsall & Trumble, 2003). Examples of a **neurosis condition** include people having abnormal feelings of anxiety or the need to obsessively check that their doors are locked.

Do you know any other fears that someone might experience if they suffered from neurosis?

. . . .

. . . .

. . . .

. . . .

. . . .

. . . .

. . . .

Someone who suffers from neurosis usually has some insight into their behaviour. 'Insight' means that they are able to see that their behaviour is unreasonable or unacceptable.

People often use the word 'psychosis' to mean angry or irrational.

What different meanings have you heard the word 'psychosis' being given?

. . . .

. . . .

. . . .

. . . .

. . . .

'Psychosis' is defined as 'a severe mental derangement, especially when resulting in delusions and loss of contact with external reality' (Pearsall & Trumble, 2003). What this means is that your ability to recognise what is real and what is imagined is seriously affected.

Schizophrenia belongs to the **psychosis disorder** and can interfere with the way you see the world around you. (Another psychotic illness is manic depression, which is moods that swing from being very high to very low.) Schizo-effective disorder is a mixture of schizo-phrenia and mood symptoms.

Some symptoms include:

- hearing 'voices'
- having jumbled thoughts
- having frightening and unusual ideas.

So if you suffer from psychosis you may hear people saying things when no one is speaking (auditory hallucinations), but they will seem very real to you.

Or you might develop a strong belief (delusion) that is not shared by others who know you well.

There are also other reasons why some people experience psychotic symptoms, for example sometimes a physical illness like a chest or urinary infection, and also a brain tumour, can cause people to experience hallucinations. These symptoms are usually only short term and are treated with either antibiotics or surgery.

Also, substance misuse, for example illegal drugs or alcohol, can cause people to experience hallucinations or psychotic symptoms. These symptoms usually disappear after a while once the sufferer stops taking these illegal substances.

Do you know of anyone who has suffered psychosis due to physical illnesses or substance misuse?

. . . .

. . . .

. . . .

. . . .

. . . .

. . . .

. . . .

. . . .

. . . .

. . . .

▶ WHAT HAVE PEOPLE SAID ABOUT SCHIZOPHRENIA?

Some people have said that schizophrenia is a 'nervous breakdown', or another word for 'madness', or that all people who suffer schizophrenia are violent. The most common myth about schizophrenia is that it is a 'split personality'.

What other negative descriptions of schizophrenia have you heard?

. . . .

. . . .

. . . .

Schizophrenia is none of these. It is not a 'Jekyll and Hyde' condition or a 'split personality', and violence is rare in schizophrenia.

How do these negative descriptions of schizophrenia above make you feel?

. . . .

. . . .

. . . .

What do you think is to blame for the general public's negative attitude?

. . . .

. . . .

. . . .

The general public's view about schizophrenia has not really kept pace with the improvements in treatment. There is still much ignorance around; however, recently there have been more sensitive portrayals on film and television of characters who suffer from schizophrenia. Furthermore, these performances have shown how the illness affects an individual in a more realistic way, demonstrating some movement in the right direction towards educating the general public.

Before you were diagnosed, what were your views on schizophrenia?

. . . .

. . . .

. . . .

. . . .

. . . .

What can be said is that schizophrenia is a condition that people develop through no fault of their own; it is a condition whereby people's thoughts, feelings and behaviour can become very disturbed and confused.

▶ HOW MANY PEOPLE IN THE UK SUFFER FROM SCHIZOPHRENIA?

Schizophrenia is said to be one of the most distressing of all mental conditions and is more common than people realise. It affects 1 in 100 people and can affect anyone, men or women, from any walk of life and in every country in the world, without taking into account their race, culture or religion (National Schizophrenia Fellowship, 2001).

How many people do you think suffer from schizophrenia in the UK?

. . . .

. . . .

. . . .

There are 51 million people worldwide who suffer from schizophrenia and currently there are over 250,000 people suffering from schizophrenia in the UK (National Institute of Mental Health, 2006).

Every year, 35,000 people are admitted to hospital in the UK with schizophrenia (Association of the British Pharmaceutical Industry, 2003).

Your illness can develop at any age, but tends to start from your mid-teens and early twenties.

What age did your illness develop?

. . . .

. . . .

What symptoms did you experience at that time?

. . . .

. . . .

. . . .

. . . .

. . . .

. . . .

. . . .

Schizophrenia does tend to occur earlier in men than women, but we are not sure why. Not only does it happen to fit and young people, it often does so without any warning.

▶ CAN YOU BE TESTED FOR SCHIZOPHRENIA?

There is no special test for schizophrenia as it is not an easy illness to recognise when it appears.

There are three reasons for this (Birchwood & Smith, 1996):

1. **Schizophrenia is a mental, and not a physical, problem; so there might be no obvious signs that something is not right.**

For example, in a physical illness some symptoms the sufferer might suffer from are:

- **pyrexia** (high temperature) and can be measured by a thermometer
- **hypertension** (high blood pressure) and can be measured by a BP machine
- **anaemia** (low red-blood-cell count) and can be measured by a blood test.

All these above ailments can be measured by doctors to diagnose certain physical illnesses.

What test could doctors do to make a diagnosis of a broken leg?

. . . .

. . . .

What test could doctors do to measure and make a diagnosis of diabetes?

. . . .

. . . .

What test could doctors do to measure and make a diagnosis of a chest infection?

. . . .

. . . .

It is not so straightforward when diagnosing schizophrenia. A doctor can only decide what illness their patient is suffering from by the unusual experiences and behaviour that their patient describes to them.

Was it an easy task for you to discuss your symptoms with your doctor?

. . . .

. . . .

2. Some people might not want to talk about the symptoms they may be experiencing.

This may be because they feel scared that others might think they are going 'mad' or that they will be admitted into hospital.

In the early days of your illness, before you saw any doctor, were you frightened by any of the symptoms you were experiencing?

. . . .

. . . .

. . . .

What did you think was wrong with you?

. . . .

. . . .

. . . .

At first, did you have any fears or anxieties about discussing your symptoms with your doctor? If so, what were they?

. . . .

. . . .

. . . .

How long was it before you were open and honest with your doctor regarding your symptoms?

. . . .

. . . .

How did you feel after talking to your doctor? Did it help?

. . . .

. . . .

. . . .

What was, or still is, your most difficult symptom you have had to discuss?

. . . .

. . . .

. . . .

Why?

. . . .

. . . .

3. **Some symptoms of schizophrenia show up gradually and often start slowly in your mid-teens.**

It can be hard for others to tell whether the gradual change in behaviour is a sign of mental illness or just normal teenage rebellion. The symptoms of schizophrenia can be similar to those of the early adolescent years.

For example, you may:

- be tired during the day and hyperactive at night
- prefer to eat alone and not with your family
- become irritable and angry with your family and others
- change your beliefs and become very religious
- smoke heavily
- self-isolate and neglect yourself
- play loud music
- find concentrating difficult
- have muddled or confusing thoughts.

Because changes can be slow, your parents won't often notice that something is wrong.

If the onset of your illness started during your adolescence, can you identify with any of the above symptoms? Which symptoms in particular? Is there anything else that is not mentioned above?

. . . .

. . . .

. . . .

. . . .

. . . .

Did this cause you to have problems with your family?

. . . .

How?

. . . .

. . . .

. . . .

So, to conclude, there is no special test for schizophrenia because doctors have to be guided by the symptoms of the illness, for example 'voices', and you need to be monitored on how you respond to certain treatment before doctors decide whether or not you suffer from schizophrenia.

▶ WHAT IS IT LIKE TO SUFFER FROM SCHIZOPHRENIA?

It is really hard to describe what it is like to suffer from schizophrenia. People talk about being constantly criticised by an unseen person. Others speak of being harassed by someone else all of the time, or of that person controlling their thoughts – and yet the sufferer never knows why this is happening, and nor can they see this other person. Worse still, it might seem obvious to the person that they are suffering in this way and yet no one else will be aware of it.

This might help non-sufferers to begin to build a picture of what it is like to suffer from schizophrenia.

Have you ever experienced any of the above or told someone about what is happening to you? Have they looked at you a bit bewildered and brushed aside what you said?

. . . .

. . . .

. . . .

Or have they looked frightened and distanced themselves from you?

. . . .

. . . .

. . . .

It is not surprising, then, that you might become withdrawn and confused.

Those who don't suffer from schizophrenia find it very hard to understand the experiences of those who do. It can be a frightening and distressing experience for families and friends to see their loved ones suffering without knowing how to help them.

How do you think your friends and family feel about your diagnosis?

. . . .

. . . .

. . . .

. . . .

. . . .

Nobody knows what schizophrenia is, except that it is an illness which affects the chemicals in the brain and that this in turn affects people's thinking, emotions and behaviour.

Some sufferers are angry or saddened when they are given a diagnosis of schizophrenia because they feel they will be stigmatised and feel bitter about the illness. Some have also said that their illness seems like a life sentence.

Did you go through similar emotions when you were told that you suffered from schizophrenia?

. . . .

. . . .

. . . .

. . . .

. . . .

. . . .

. . . .

. . . .

. . . .

. . . .

. . . .

. . . .

. . . .

But then some sufferers are relieved to be given a diagnosis of schizophrenia because it makes them realise that they are not alone in their troubles and that the condition is treatable and that help is at hand.

How does the above statement make you feel?

. . . .

. . . .

. . . .

. . . .

. . . .

. . . .

. . . .

. . . .

After completing these sessions, it is hoped that you will have a better understanding of your illness, enabling you to focus less on the negative aspects of your condition and more on working towards leading a normal and positive life.

Do you agree with your doctor that you suffer from schizophrenia?

. . . .

. . . .

. . . .

. . . .

If not, what do you think you are suffering from?

. . . .

. . . .

. . . .

. . . .

. . . .

. . . .

You may not agree with your doctor's diagnosis, but please continue to work through this workbook with an open frame of mind, making a decision only at the end of the six sessions, that is after you have been made fully aware of all the facts first.

▶ **End-of-session Questionnaire**

What three important things have you learnt and will take away with you from Session 1 (you may need to browse through the session again to jog your memory)?

1) . . . .
. . . .
. . . .
. . . .
. . . .
. . . .
. . . .
. . . .
. . . .
. . . .

2) . . . .
. . . .
. . . .
. . . .
. . . .
. . . .
. . . .
. . . .
. . . .

3) . . . .
. . . .
. . . .
. . . .
. . . .
. . . .
. . . .
. . . .

▶ Questionnaire

These questions are not meant to be seen as a test. They are only a means of sharing information and getting you to think about your illness before you start your session. If you're not sure, just make a guess: there are no right or wrong answers.

1. Do you think schizophrenia is inherited?

2. Do you think that stress can cause schizophrenia?

3. Do you know of anyone who has taken illegal drugs and then developed a mental illness?

Session 2

During this session we will be looking at the most frequently asked questions about the causes of schizophrenia:

1. Can you inherit schizophrenia?

2. Does stress cause schizophrenia?

3. Do illegal drugs cause schizophrenia?

Session 2

At present, no one can find a single reason as to what causes schizophrenia, but there is likely to be a number of triggers involved and really there is no knowing who will develop the illness.

Some explanations have been put forward, as will be discussed below, but no one knows for sure what causes schizophrenia.

▶ CAN YOU INHERIT SCHIZOPHRENIA?

Most people who develop schizophrenia do not have a family member with this sort of illness, but in some cases schizophrenia does run in families.

Does a member of your family also suffer from schizophrenia?

. . . .

Nine out of 10 people who develop schizophrenia will be the first in their family to do so (Birchwood & Smith, 1996).

The risks of developing schizophrenia are:	
No family history	1%
Brother or sister has schizophrenia	9%
One parent who has schizophrenia	12%
Both parents have schizophrenia	40%
Identical twins (one affected)	25–50%
Non-identical twins (one affected)	10%

(Leff, 1996, p.5)

Identical twins have identical genes (carrier of heredity); so if schizophrenia was due *only* to inheritance we would expect that if one twin had schizophrenia then the other twin also would have the illness.

What are your feelings regarding the percentage risk and hereditary factors mentioned above?

. . . .

. . . .

. . . .

. . . .

Just because one member of your family has developed schizophrenia does not mean that others in the family will develop it also.

Do you think this percentage of risks might make a difference when deciding to have children of your own?

. . . .

. . . .

. . . .

The above-mentioned figures should not deter you from having children if you would like to. Because you suffer from schizophrenia, the risks are a 12% chance that your child will also suffer from the same illness.

But that also means there is an 88% chance that your children will not develop schizophrenia.

How does this make you feel?

. . . .

. . . .

. . . .

. . . .

. . . .

Also, if your child develops schizophrenia, the advantages of being a parent with the same illness is that you are more likely to become familiar with the symptoms earlier and seek help.

So there is no reason why people suffering from schizophrenia should not have children if they want to.

▶ DOES STRESS CAUSE SCHIZOPHRENIA?

Each one of us has our own level of tolerating situations and changes that life can bring along, but when circumstances become particularly difficult, we describe our experience as 'being stressed'.

There are all sorts of situations that can be stressful, and stress affects anyone and everyone. Some of the most important areas of our life for causing stress are:

- pressure at work
- problems with family
- money worries
- relationship problems
- accommodation problems
- pain due to physical problems.

What has caused you to feel stressed in the past?

. . . .

. . . .

. . . .

Stress can cause both physical and mental symptoms, i.e. butterflies in your stomach and poor concentration.

There are some physical problems that are brought on by stress, which could lead to:

- high blood pressure
- stomach ulcers
- headaches
- sexual dysfunction.

Can you think of other physical ailments that are brought on by stress?

. . . .

. . . .

. . . .

Stress obviously affects us mentally as well and could lead to:

- anxiety
- depression.

However, the effects of stress usually clear up with time, but if we can work out what caused our stress and how it affects us personally we can then take positive steps to manage it.

Some people who suffer from schizophrenia have experienced some difficult stresses prior to the first episode of their illness. This might be:

- moving house
- exams
- bereavement.

Were there any main stressful factors prior to your illness?

. . . .

. . . .

. . . .

. . . .

> **Stress cannot be the cause of schizophrenia, but it may trigger the illness.**

Some people cope differently under stress. Some *unhelpful* coping strategies are:

- smoking
- excessive use of alcohol
- use of illegal drugs
- irritability with others
- angry outbursts.

How do you usually cope in stressful situations?

....

....

....

....

....

....

Would you like to learn more coping strategies. If so, why?

....

....

....

....

....

....

> **Stress is also known to cause sufferers a relapse in their schizophrenia.**

Have you experienced any relapses or episodes of deterioration in your illness?

....

If so, was stress a factor?

....

....

....

....

....

We cannot avoid stress in our lives, because it is part of normal everyday living, but it should be emphasised that you must *not* be afraid of stress in the case of relapses.

It is very important that you learn skills on how to cope with stress more effectively, which would help prevent you from any future relapses.

> **Remember that stress does not cause schizophrenia, but it can trigger an attack and make the symptoms worse, causing a relapse.**

There now follow some suggestions to help you cope with stress more effectively.

STRESS

Stress can be described as tension, anxiety, pressure, worry and strain. It has an enormous impact on how you feel. The important thing for you to remember is that *too much* stress can lead to a crisis, or a relapse in your illness, and that you need to learn how to cope more effectively in situations that cause you to feel stressed.

One way of dealing with situations when stressful events happen is for you to change the outcome, to a more positive or manageable one.

Below are some ways of coping when faced with stressful situations. These include changing the way you think and feel when stressed and strategies on how to cope when you physically respond to stress.

If a situation seems stressful to you

You can *change the outcome* of a stressful situation by learning to be more assertive and by improving your negotiation and time-management skills.

For example, you have a friend who wants to always tag along with you, but at times you feel that you want some space on your own. You are in a rush to get to your doctor's appointment and your friend asks if they can come along as you are about to go out of the door, which makes you feel frustrated and irritated with your friend.

What could you do or say in this situation that would make you feel less stressed? (Refer to the above statement regarding how you can change the outcome.)

. . . .

. . . .

. . . .

. . . .

Effectively communicating your needs and sticking up for yourself will help others understand you.

[If you need more help in learning these skills, speak to your key nurse.]

If it's the way you think about the situation that causes you stress

You can *change your thoughts* to see things differently by using positive self-talk or humour.

For example, you are very worried that your friend will think badly of you but don't want to fall out with them as you consider them to be a good friend.

How else could you change your thoughts so that you see this situation differently and in a way that would make you feel less stressed? (Refer to the above statement on how you can change your thoughts.)

. . . .

. . . .

. . . .

. . . .

. . . .

. . . .

. . . .

. . . .

Stress causes us to think in a negative way, but monitoring our thoughts will help us see what is happening in a rational way.

Use self-calming statements like 'Don't take it personally' and 'I have a right to have time on my own if I want to'.

Also, being able to lighten up a situation with humour can make it less overwhelming.
[If you need more help in learning these skills, speak to your key nurse.]

If it's the way you feel about a situation that causes you stress

You can *change your emotions* to feel different, using positive self-talk or by talking it over with the person involved or someone close to you.

For example, you feel very guilty that you may have hurt your friend's feelings regarding the situation and feel insecure about your relationship.

How else could you change your feelings so that you see this situation differently that would help you feel less stressed? (Refer to the above statement on how you can change your emotions.)

. . . .

. . . .

. . . .

. . . .

. . . .

. . . .

. . . .

. . . .

Talking to supportive friends, relatives and professionals can help and change your view on the situation.

They do say a problem shared is a problem halved.

[If you need more help in learning these skills, speak to your key nurse.]

If it's the way your body responds to a situation that causes you stress

You can change the way your *body releases tension* by relaxation techniques and talking it over with someone close to you.

While you are thinking about this stressful situation, you can feel your heart beating faster and the tension in your muscles. How could you release the tension in your body, which would make this situation less stressful? (Refer to the above statement on how you can change the way your body releases tension.)

. . . .

. . . .

. . . .

. . . .

. . . .

. . . .

. . . .

. . . .

Relaxing the mind and body will help take away any physical and psychological tension.

[If you need more help in learning these skills, speak to your keyworker.]

Here are some **helpful coping strategies** to relieve stress and keep you feeling well:

- listening to music
- watching TV
- having a bath
- writing your thoughts in a diary
- exercising or playing sports
- doing relaxation techniques
- using humour and laughter
- problem-solving by breaking the problem down into manageable parts
- enjoying a healthy diet and adequate sleep
- distraction, e.g. counting from 1 to 10
- self-praise for remaining in control
- focusing on the task in hand
- doing some gardening
- visiting places of interest to you
- attending a centre
- visiting friends and family
- painting or drawing a picture

Here are some more **not so helpful coping strategies** that you might do if you feel stressed:

- smoking
- using illegal drugs or alcohol to cope
- avoiding the problems
- taking it out on others
- isolating yourself and not wanting to be around others
- denying that you have problems
- being overactive and very busy
- over-eating or under-eating
- self-harming

Which would make a positive outcome to a stressful situation more likely: the helpful or the unhelpful coping strategies?

Which of the above have you usually done when you have felt stressed?

. . . .

. . . .

. . . .

. . . .

. . . .

Think of a time recently when you felt stressed and then complete the stress diary below:

Example of a Stress Diary

Time and day

. . . .

Briefly describe what happened

. . . .

. . . .

. . . .

. . . .

Identify the emotions you felt and, on a scale of 0–10 (zero = very weakly and 10 = very strongly), rate them according to how strongly or not you felt each emotion.

. . . .

. . . .

. . . .

What thoughts went through your mind?

. . . .

. . . .

. . . .

Which coping strategies did you use to handle the stress?

. . . .

. . . .

. . . .

Did they work?

. . . .

If not, why do you think they did not work?

. . . .

. . . .

. . . .

If your coping strategies did not work, what could you have done differently?

. . . .

. . . .

. . . .

. . . .

Photocopy the above and complete every week

Understanding Your Schizophrenia Illness: A Workbook, Chris Healy,
© 2007, John Wiley & Sons, Ltd

▶ DO ILLEGAL DRUGS CAUSE SCHIZOPHRENIA?

Sometimes the use of illegal drugs, for example ecstasy (E), LSD (acid), amphetamines (speed) and cannabis (hash, pot, ganja, skunk, dope, spliffs and joints) and other illegal drugs, seem to bring on the symptoms of schizophrenia. There also seems to be overwhelming evidence regarding a link between cannabis and developing schizophrenia (Doughty, 2006).

It has been said that cannabis users are six times more likely to develop schizophrenia, especially if they are using cannabis before the age of 18 (Chapman, 2002)

Hence, research has concluded that:

> The younger you are when you first try cannabis, and the stronger it is, the more likely it is that you develop a psychotic illness, such as schizophrenia.
>
> Cannabis contains high levels of THC (Tetrahydrocannabinol, a psychoactive compound), which disrupts the chemical balance of the brain.

Have you ever taken illegal drugs in the past?

. . . .

If yes, which illegal drugs have you taken?

. . . .

. . . .

. . . .

. . . .

. . . .

. . . .

If you used cannabis, how does the above research information make you feel?

. . . .

. . . .

. . . .

. . . .

. . . .

. . . .

. . . .

Do you know of anyone, for example friends, who have taken illegal drugs and have experienced any of the symptoms that were similar to schizophrenia? Describe what they experienced.

. . . .

. . . .

. . . .

Do you know if they later developed schizophrenia?

. . . .

The following seven questions are for those sufferers who use illegal drugs.

If you used illegal drugs, did you take them as a form of self-medication (to help you to cope with your disturbing symptoms)?

. . . .

If so, which symptoms in particular did they help with?

. . . .

. . . .

. . . .

. . . .

How did taking illegal drugs help?

. . . .

. . . .

. . . .

. . . .

Do think that you should stop taking illegal drugs?

. . . .

Why?

. . . .

. . . .

. . . .

. . . .

Do you think it might be difficult for you to stop taking illegal drugs?

. . . .

Do you need help to stay away from illegal drugs?

. . . .

WHY YOU SHOULD NOT TAKE ILLEGAL DRUGS

There are a number of reasons why people use illegal drugs, and chief among them is that they enjoy the experience, but people also take drugs out of curiosity, to rebel and also because of peer pressure. If you have used illegal drugs, what were the reasons why you became involved in them?

. . . .

. . . .

. . . .

As already mentioned, if you take illegal drugs while suffering from schizophrenia, it will cause many problems for you. It will affect the way you see normal everyday things and also affect your behaviour.

Most illegal drugs cause mainly distressing feelings of persecution (paranoia); other experiences are restlessness, insomnia and depression.

Taking illegal drugs (or alcohol abuse) might:

- encourage your psychotic symptoms to come back or your present symptoms to get worse
- cause you to have arguments with your family, or you may even lose your family
- cause distressing withdrawal symptoms when you try to stop taking them
- interfere with your medication, making some side effects worse
- make you depressed or suicidal
- make holding down a job or keeping your friends difficult
- physically damage your stomach and liver
- mean you lose the trust of everyone around you
- make you lose your self-respect
- make preventing a relapse in your illness difficult, if not impossible
- make you feel better in the short term, but the long-term damage can be considerable
- cost you a lot of money
- make you commit a crime.

If you have used illegal drugs, what problems have they caused you?

. . . .

. . . .

. . . .

. . . .

. . . .

. . . .

. . . .

. . . .

. . . .

Saying 'no' to illegal drugs would mean:

- your mind will be more rational
- you will be in better health
- you will be able to nip a relapse in the bud or hold it back
- there will be less risk of losing your job or friends
- you will have more money in your pocket
- your family will be more trusting towards you
- you will be more on your guard to any psychotic symptoms
- you will have a happier relationship with your family
- you won't have a criminal record
- you can get on with your life
- you will be able to have more control over your illness
- your memory will be much better.

Of the above list, what things would be important to you if you said 'no' to illegal drugs?

. . . .

. . . .

. . . .

. . . .

. . . .

. . . .

If you think that you do not suffer from schizophrenia but believe that your symptoms are a drug-induced psychosis, what has caused you to think this?

. . . .

. . . .

. . . .

. . . .

. . . .

. . . .

Do you from time to time suffer from symptoms that are much like the symptoms you experience when taking illegal drugs (e.g. paranoia)?

. . . .

. . . .

. . . .

If you do, how do you explain this if you are not taking illegal drugs now?

. . . .

. . . .

. . . .

Are you finding it difficult coming to terms with having a diagnosis of schizophrenia?

. . . .

If you are feeling like this, it is understandable, but you must speak to your doctor or key-worker about your feelings regarding this.

If you suffer from schizophrenia and have an illegal drug or alcohol problem, mental health professionals will say that you suffer from a 'dual diagnosis' (Rethink, 2006).

So, to recap, what do you **gain** by **taking** illegal drugs?

. . . .

. . . .

. . . .

. . . .

And what do you **gain** by **not taking** illegal drugs?

. . . .

. . . .

. . . .

. . . .

Also what do you **lose** by **taking** illegal drugs?

. . . .

. . . .

. . . .

. . . .

. . . .

What do you **lose** by **not taking** illegal drugs?

. . . .

. . . .

. . . .

. . . .

> **What can be more important than your mental health and well-being?**

> **You only have one life: make it worthwhile and meaningful.**

▶ **End-of-session Questionnaire**

What three important things have you learnt and will take away with you from Session 2 (you may need to browse through the session again to jog your memory)?

1) ....

....

....

....

....

....

....

....

....

....

2) ....

....

....

....

....

....

....

....

....

....

3) ....

....

....

....

....

....

....

....

....

Session 3

▶ Questionnaire

These questions are not meant to be seen as a test. They are only a means of sharing information and getting you to think about your illness before you start your session. If you are not sure, just make a guess: there are no right or wrong answers.

1. What did you learn at school about your brain?

2. What have you heard that causes schizophrenia?

3. Do you know any famous person that suffers from schizophrenia?

Session 3

During this section, we will be looking at some of the most frequently asked questions regarding the cause of schizophrenia.

1. Is schizophrenia something to do with the brain?

2. What does *not* cause schizophrenia?

3. Do famous people suffer from schizophrenia?

Session 3

▶ **IS SCHIZOPHRENIA SOMETHING TO DO WITH THE BRAIN?**

What did you learn at school about your brain?

....

....

....

....

The brain has some incredible tasks:

- It controls your body temperature, blood pressure, heart rate and breathing.
- It takes in information received via your eyes, nose, ears etc. about what is going on around you.
- It deals with all of your physical movements, like walking, talking, sitting or standing.
- It lets you think, dream and experience emotions.

And all of this is done by your brain.

The brain and the rest of the nervous system are made up of many different cells, but the main nerve cell is called a **neurone**.

All sensations (tasting chocolate), movements (jumping up and down), thoughts (I must wash my hair), memories (your first day at school) and feelings (I am happy) are the result of signals that pass through these neurones.

Give other examples of:

sensations (hear, see, taste, touch, smell) ....

movements ....

thoughts ....

feelings ....

All of these are the results of neurones passing information to each other.

How many neurones do you think we might need to do all of this work?

....

We are born with millions of neurones that have the ability to gather and transmit electrochemical signals or messages – just like the circuits in a computer (Marieb, 1989).

Scientists have learnt a lot about these neurones, or nerve cells, by studying the **synapse**. A synapse is a small gap that separates one nerve cell from another. This is the place where information gets passed from one nerve cell to the next nerve cell with the help of special chemicals called **neurotransmitters** (Marieb, 1989).

It is here where it is thought that the brain may play a role in schizophrenia. It is said that sufferers produce too much of one of these chemicals. This chemical is called **dopamine** and the medication that helps to control the symptoms of schizophrenia seems to help reduce the level of dopamine.

These changes in the dopamine levels cause the nerves that carry information from the eyes, ears, nose and skin to become confused and bewildered. This can make the person see, hear, smell and feel things that are not actually there (have hallucinations; see pp. 42–46) or think things that those around them regard as false or irrational (have delusions; see pp. 46–51).

Other chemicals and brain receptors may be affected, but more research is on the way to find out the cause of schizophrenia.

What other explanations have you been given as to what causes schizophrenia?

. . . .

. . . .

. . . .

Besides the increase of dopamine levels in the brain, and this being one of the main explanations for schizophrenia, there have been other theories:

> ■ enlargement of the ventricles in the brain
> ■ inherited from their parents
> ■ minor injuries at birth
> ■ mother contracting a virus
> ■ illegal drug-taking and in particular cannabis (Chapman, 2002)
> ■ faulty chromosome (gene) (National Institute of Mental Health, 2004)

None of these ideas is able to provide a complete answer about the triggers of schizophrenia, but many psychiatrists say that schizophrenia is caused by a combination of factors, that is:

> **Perhaps a person's genetic make-up makes them vulnerable to developing schizophrenia, which is triggered by environmental events, for example stress or illegal drugs.**

Have you understood the link between increased dopamine levels and schizophrenia?

. . . .

Can you explain this theory in your own words?

. . . .

. . . .

. . . .

. . . .

. . . .

. . . .

. . . .

. . . .

. . . .

If you are unable to fully understand the link between increased dopamine and your illness, you need to learn more about it by speaking to your doctor or keyworker before you continue on to the next session

▶ WHAT DOES *NOT* CAUSE SCHIZOPHRENIA?

What we do know is that many suggestions can be ruled out as causing schizophrenia. These include:

- your family life and upbringing
- low intelligence
- your personality.

It has not been proved that difficult relationships within a family can trigger a schizophrenic illness. But families can play an important role in preventing their relative from having a relapse.

What are your own personal thoughts on what causes schizophrenia?

. . . .

. . . .

. . . .

. . . .

. . . .

. . . .

. . . .

. . . .

. . . .

▶ DO FAMOUS PEOPLE SUFFER FROM SCHIZOPHRENIA?

Syd Barrett	of the band Pink Floyd
Eduard Einstein	Son of Albert Einstein
Andy Goram	A Scottish soccer goalkeeper who played for Rangers
James Beck Gordon	Drummer in the 1960s and 1970s
Peter Green	Guitarist for the band Fleetwood Mac
Mary Todd Lincoln	Wife of former US president Abraham Lincoln
John Nash	Mathematician and Nobel Prize winner in 1994. A blockbuster film, *A Beautiful Mind*, in 2001 emphasises his struggle with schizophrenia
Vaslav Nijinsky	Russian ballet dancer
Nancy Spungen	Girlfriend of Sid Vicious from the punk rock band The Sex Pistols.

(Schizophrenia.com, 2006)

Did you know or are you surprised that these people suffered from schizophrenia?

....

....

....

....

....

....

....

....

....

....

....

....

....

Has learning that some famous people have had the same illness as you made you think differently about the label 'schizophrenia'?

. . . .

. . . .

. . . .

. . . .

. . . .

. . . .

. . . .

. . . .

. . . .

. . . .

. . . .

. . . .

. . . .

Has learning how some famous people have managed to cope and remain successful despite their illness made you think differently about your illness?

. . . .

. . . .

. . . .

. . . .

. . . .

. . . .

. . . .

. . . .

. . . .

. . . .

. . . .

. . . .

. . . .

. . . .

. . . .

▶ **End-of-session Questionnaire**

What three important things have you learnt and will take away with you from Session 3?
(You may need to browse through the session again to jog your memory.)

1) . . . .
. . . .
. . . .
. . . .
. . . .
. . . .
. . . .
. . . .
. . . .
. . . .

2) . . . .
. . . .
. . . .
. . . .
. . . .
. . . .
. . . .
. . . .
. . . .

3) . . . .
. . . .
. . . .
. . . .
. . . .
. . . .
. . . .
. . . .
. . . .

Session 4

These questions are not meant to be seen as a test. They are only a means of sharing information and getting you to think about your illness before you start your session. If you're not sure, just make a guess: there are no right or wrong answers.

1. What does the word 'hallucination' mean to you? Can you give an example that you, or maybe someone you know, have experienced?

2. What does the word 'delusion' mean to you? Can you give an example that you, or maybe someone you know, have experienced?

3. Have you heard the term 'negative and positive symptoms'? What is your understanding of this?

4. List the symptoms of your illness.

5. How did these symptoms make you feel?

▶ WHAT ARE THE SYMPTOMS?

Recognising schizophrenia is not always easy as there may be no obvious signs. Your symptoms may take a while to show and you may not want to talk to anyone about what you are going through.

As already mentioned in Session 1, we can recognise the symptoms of some illnesses, for example 'a cold' (that is a cough, high temperature and sneezing).

But do you know the symptoms of Lyme disease or muscular dystrophy? Most likely you don't, and when you first became ill with schizophrenia you also probably did not recognise the symptoms.

What were the first symptoms you suffered from, or an unusual experience you had, that made you realise that something was not 'quite right' with you?

. . . .

. . . .

. . . .

. . . .

. . . .

. . . .

. . . .

How long did it take you to realise that you were unwell?

. . . .

It can take some people months or even years before they seek any treatment.

In the initial stages of your illness you will be very frightened and anxious because you will not know what is wrong with you and so will not be familiar with the symptoms of schizophrenia or be aware that you are suffering from this illness.

People with schizophrenia can be affected in different ways, and no two people will experience the same symptoms. However, symptoms normally cause the sufferer's understanding of the world around them to change, altering their **behaviour**, **thinking** and **feelings**.

So what are the symptoms?

The most common symptoms are:

- **delusions** (a false belief): such as thinking that people are conspiring against you when they are not (this is called 'paranoia') or that you believe you are someone famous (this is called 'grandiosity')
- **hallucinations:** hearing voices that no one else can hear or seeing, smelling, tasting or feeling things that are not there
- **passivity experiences:** believing that objects, events or people can control your thoughts in a way that cannot be explained
- **withdrawal** from social contact and having trouble washing and dressing yourself

You may hear doctors talking about the **positive and negative symptoms** of schizophrenia. Have you heard this term?

. . . .

These symptoms are usually divided into two types:
> A **positive symptom** is usually one that is *added* to a person's thinking, that was not there before (Birchwood & Smith, 1996).

Can you think of an example?

. . . .

An example of this might be hearing 'voices'. This is something that you might have now that was not there before the diagnosis of your illness and **should not be there.**

A **negative symptom** is usually one that is *lost* from a person's usual experience or behaviour (Birchwood & Smith, 1996).
Can you think of an example?

. . . .

An example of this might be a sudden lack of interest in mixing with other people. This is something that you may **have done** before and which **should be there.**

Positive and **negative** symptoms *do not mean* **good** and **bad** symptoms

There are two types of symptoms, not two types of schizophrenia.

Positive symptoms	Negative symptoms
hallucinations	lack of motivation
delusions	lack of self care
paranoid beliefs	lose the ability of being able to enjoy experiences as
disordered thinking	before 'blunt affect'

We will discuss these symptoms in more detail further on in this session. All this must have been very frightening and worrying for you, trying to understand what was happening to you. Also, because your illness changes the way you see the whole world, you may have lost touch with what was really happening to you.

Can you remember if you were afraid and confused about what was happening to you when you experienced any of the negative or positive symptoms mentioned?

. . . .

. . . .

. . . .

. . . .

. . . .

. . . .

. . . .

Do you think that at some point in your illness you lost touch with reality, that is you were unable to separate real from unreal experiences or that your understanding of what was happening to you was not shared by others?

....

....

....

....

....

....

It's possible to cope with these difficult and distressing symptoms, and further on in these sessions we will explore how you can deal with them.

It can sometimes be distressing and difficult talking about your symptoms, but hopefully, with the support of your keyworker working through this workbook with you, it won't be such a difficult task.

Although it might be difficult at first, it is hoped that when you have understood what it is that you are going through you will be able to make sense of your experiences and learn some skills so that you will be able to manage your distressing symptoms more effectively.

One of the positive symptoms of schizophrenia is **hallucinations**, which we will now discuss.

HALLUCINATIONS

Hallucinations can take a number of different forms. They can be:

- auditory
- visual
- tactile
- olfactory
- gustatory

Auditory hallucinations – hearing things, for example voices, when no one is around.

This will be discussed in more detail further on in this session.

Have you or anyone you know experienced any auditory hallucinations?

....

....

....

....

Visual hallucinations – seeing things that are not there.

For example, some people who suffer from this type of positive symptom might believe that they have seen a vision of God or the Virgin Mary.

Have you or anyone you know experienced any visual hallucinations?

. . . .

. . . .

. . . .

. . . .

Tactile hallucinations – feeling things that other people do not feel or believing something is touching you when it is not.

Some people who suffer from this type of positive symptom may, for example, feel the sensation of insects crawling on them.

Have you or anyone you know experienced any tactile hallucinations?

. . . .

. . . .

. . . .

. . . .

. . . .

Olfactory hallucinations – smelling odours and scents that other people cannot smell.

Some people who suffer from this type of positive symptom may, for example, complain of smelling unpleasant things, like excrement.

Have you or anyone you know experienced olfactory hallucinations?

. . . .

. . . .

. . . .

. . . .

. . . .

Gustatory hallucinations – tasting something that is not there.

Some people who suffer from this positive symptom complain that their food tastes different and also sometimes feel that their food has been tampered with or that they are being poisoned.

Have you or anyone you know experienced any gustatory hallucinations?

. . . .

. . . .

. . . .

. . . .

. . . .

Auditory hallucinations

Auditory hallucinations are the most common type of hallucination and in this session we will look at them in more detail.

'Voices' is hearing others talking when no one else is around, or when nobody seems to be saying the words you hear.

Unless someone has experienced these symptoms, it is difficult to appreciate how frightening it can be to hear 'voices'. This is a real experience for those who suffer from it and is not imagined.

Before we discuss the four types of 'voices', we need to understand that 'voices' can:

- be either male, female or both
- refer to you by name
- be funny
- be supportive
- be critical
- be abusive
- say personal stuff about you that only you know
- tell you to do things which you might not want to do
- be threatening
- be more than one voice
- sound like people you know
- sound like people you don't know
- sometimes feel as if they are coming from your neighbours or from people you pass in the street
- make you laugh
- call you nasty names
- be nice to you and give you good advice
- comment on what you are thinking.

Which of the above 'voices' have you experienced?

. . . .

. . . .

. . . .

. . . .

. . . .

. . . .

There are four types of auditory hallucination (Stuttaford & Sharma, 1999):

1. 'voices' heard in the second person
2. 'voices' heard in the third person
3. 'voices' heard like a running commentary
4. 'voices' heard like a thought echo

■ The 'voices' can be heard in the 'second person'

An example of this is that it seems as if the 'voices' are talking directly to you. They can say nice things to you ('You are clever') or say awful things to you ('You are lazy').

■ The 'voice' can be heard in the 'third person'

An example of this is when you feel aware that someone is discussing you in general, as if you were not there. The 'voice' seems to be talking to someone else or another 'voice', and this might seem that you are overhearing a conversation about you.

To make sense of this, you might think that the TV or radio is referring to you and because this information is personal to you it can be very puzzling and difficult for you to understand why this should happen.

■ The 'voices' are heard like a 'running commentary'

An example of this is 'He should not have done that' or 'Now she is going to bed'.

■ 'Voices' can be heard like a 'thought echo'

It feels like your inner voice has the ability to echo your own thoughts, which your 'voice' then repeats.

Hearing 'voices' can be very upsetting, especially if they are critical or abusive – as they often seem to be.

'Voices' are heard through the ears and so appear to be very real and can seem to be coming from thin air. As already mentioned, you may hear them coming from the TV and may try to find an explanation for them. For example, you might think there are hidden microphones or loud speakers in your house that are being used by other people to spy on or contact you, or that you are connected to a spirit world in some way.

Have you or someone you know experienced any of the four types of auditory hallucination mentioned above? If so, which ones?

. . . .

. . . .

. . . .

How did you make sense of what was happening to you?

. . . .

. . . .

. . . .

. . . .

Some people with schizophrenia believe that auditory hallucinations are real. 'Voices' are not imagined, but they are created by your own mind: the brain can mistake your own thoughts for real voices (Royal College of Psychiatrists, 2003).

Do you still from time to time suffer from auditory hallucinations?

. . . .

. . . .

. . . .

If so, how do you cope?

. . . .

. . . .

. . . .

. . . .

If you are able to recognise any of these positive symptoms above, it might be helpful to know there are a variety of ways in which you can lessen the effects of the 'voices' and to learn how to cope with them better. This will be discussed in Session 6.

Another positive symptom is delusion, which we will discuss next. It can be distressing and difficult talking about your symptoms, but it is hoped that progressing through this workbook with your keyworker will make the process easier.

Although it will be difficult at first, when you have understood what it is that you have been going through you will be able to make sense of your experiences and also learn skills so that you will be able to manage your distressing symptoms more effectively.

DELUSIONS

A delusion is a belief that you hold with complete confidence but that, while you have no doubt that your belief is real, other people may see as untrue or strange.

Your delusions will cause you to have thoughts and experiences that no one else has, and this in turn will cause you some difficulty when trying to discuss your beliefs with others. This is because your reasons do not make sense to them and sometimes you cannot explain it yourself.

For example, you may believe that:

- people are against you and you may fear that others may do you harm
- you have special powers
- your body and mind are under the control of some outside force or power
- people are talking to you on the radio or through the TV.

A delusion may sometimes come out of the blue, and often after a few weeks or months where you have felt there has been some odd happenings but could not find an explanation for them.

Has this ever happened to you?

. . . .

You may develop a delusional idea as a way of explaining, for example, hallucinations or other strange experiences. Because they seem so real, you feel that you have to find some reason for them. For example, if you heard 'voices' talking about you and describing what you were doing, you might decide that you were being monitored and spied on by the Government.

Has this ever happened to you?

. . . .

Delusions take on many forms and are divided up into:

1. delusions of reference
2. somatic delusions
3. delusions of control
4. grandiose delusions
5. paranoid or persecutory delusions

Delusions of reference

With this type of delusion, you may start to see special meanings into ordinary, everyday things and might really believe that they are specially connected to you.

For example, as we have already mentioned, you might believe people are talking about you, including people on the radio or television and you may feel that these people are trying to connect with you in some way. You might also feel that it could be 'God'.

This is because your illness causes you to think this way. It makes sense and is real to you, but not to others. This causes you to feel misunderstood by others, and when your experiences are frightening it can be a very difficult and confusing time for you.

Have you, or someone you know, suffered from delusions of reference ?

....

....

....

....

....

....

....

....

....

Somatic delusions

Somatic delusions are false beliefs about your body. You may feel you have a terrible illness or that something strange is in your body.

You might have real worries about your health and be convinced that the everyday aches and pains that most people suffer from now and again are more life-threatening than what your doctor says.

Have you, or someone you know, suffered from somatic delusions?

....

....

....

....

Delusions of control

This type of delusion is the belief that your whole body and mind are under the influence of some outside force or power, for example the Devil, God, spirits or witchcraft. You might feel that your thoughts are being taken out of your mind. Or you might feel that your thoughts are not your own and that someone has put them there.

Have you, or someone you know, suffered from delusions of control?

....

....

....

....

....

· ·

· ·

· ·

· ·

Grandiose delusions

If you suffer from this delusion, you might believe that you are famous or an important figure; you might also believe you are special, for example 'like God's special messenger' or the second Jesus Christ. Also with this symptom you might also believe you have special powers or abilities.

Delusional beliefs often have a religious context where the sufferer believes that they are hearing the word of God (Chadwick, 2000).

Have you, or someone you know, suffered from grandiose delusions?

· ·

Paranoid or persecutory delusions

Paranoia is the most common delusion; a third of people with schizophrenia often have delusions of a persecutory nature, that is an unshakable belief that they are harassed, conspired against or that people are 'out to get them'. Some sufferers also believe that their friends or family are against them and that they wish them some harm.

Have you, or someone you know, experienced paranoid/persecutory delusions?

· ·

· ·

· ·

You might feel that others are plotting against you and this may have caused you to be preoccupied with uncovering their (whoever you feel is plotting against you) 'conspiracy'.

These thoughts are sometimes reinforced by auditory hallucinations (see p. 44), which could be described as a coping mechanism used by the sufferer to make sense of what they are experiencing.

Ideas that make you feel persecuted or suspicious may be:

- out-of-the-ordinary paranoid ideas: you may believe that the Government is spying on you or that you are being influenced by neighbours who are using some equipment to monitor you
- everyday paranoid ideas: you may believe that your spouse is unfaithful or that people don't like you or want to punish or harm you (Royal College of Psychiatrists, 2003).

Have you, or someone you know, experienced out-of-the-ordinary or everyday paranoid delusions?

. . . .

. . . .

. . . .

It is said that those suffering from paranoid delusions have a low self-esteem and that this symptom is a defence mechanism or a form of self-protection. It is also said that some people see themselves as being bad or see others as bad (Chadwick *et al.*, 1996).

Would you say this is true of yourself?

. . . .

If you suffered from any of the delusions mentioned, how did you make sense of what was happening to you?

. . . .

. . . .

. . . .

. . . .

. . . .

. . . .

. . . .

These symptoms can be quite worrying and frustrating, and it is sometimes difficult for you to make sense of your experiences. It also may cause friction between you and your family, friends and health professionals because they do not share the same beliefs as you.

Has this happened to you?

. . . .

. . . .

. . . .

. . . .

Do you still from time to time suffer from these symptoms?

. . . .

. . . .

. . . .

. . . .

. . . .

. . . .

. . . .

How do they make you feel?

. . . .

. . . .

. . . .

. . . .

. . . .

. . . .

. . . .

How do you cope?

. . . .

. . . .

. . . .

. . . .

These positive symptoms can make you feel lonely and misunderstood, but it might be helpful to know that there are a variety of ways of coping with these beliefs, which will be discussed in Session 6.

NEGATIVE SYMPTOMS

Negative symptoms are less obvious than positive ones:

- You can't concentrate or think straight.
- You can't be bothered to get up, and spend most of your time in your room.
- You find it difficult to wash or keep yourself clean and are unable to cope with everyday tasks, like tidying the house.
- You can't be bothered to go down the shops.
- You want to avoid people, and you even find it difficult to be in the company of family or friends.
- Your interest in life and finding enjoyment in things is not there like it used to be.
- You feel emotional numbness and don't seen to laugh much anymore.
- Your thoughts wander off, and you cannot concentrate on a conversation for too long before you are distracted.
- You lack confidence in a conversation because you feel that you have nothing to contribute.
- You distance yourself from others and avoid any eye contact.
- You lose the ability to show emotion at the right time and may laugh at things that are sad.
- You often have a blank facial expression.
- You have low energy levels and tend to sit around and sleep more than usual.
- You tend to get wrapped up in yourself and are not bothered whether you have friends or not.
- You cannot be bothered to pursue any hobbies.

If you suffered from any of the negative symptoms, it must have been hard for you to explain to your family how you felt. These symptoms seem to irritate families more than positive symptoms do, and they tend to accuse the sufferer of being lazy. But it is hard for them to understand that these are the symptoms of your illness

Which of the above negative symptoms have you experienced?

. . . .

. . . .

. . . .

. . . .

. . . .

The newer atypical medication has helped a lot to reduce these distressing negative symptoms.

▶ End-of-session Questionnaire

What three important things have you learnt and will take away with you from Session 4 (you may need to browse through the session again to jog your memory)?

1) ....
....
....
....
....
....
....
....
....
....
....

2) ....
....
....
....
....
....
....
....
....
....
....

3) ....
....
....
....
....
....
....
....
....
....

Session 5

Questionnaire

These questions are not meant to be seen as a test. They are only a means of sharing information and getting you to think about your illness before you start your session. If you're not sure, just make a guess: there are no right or wrong answers.

1. What medication are you taking at the moment?

2. Why do you take it?

3. What side effects, if any, have you experienced from taking your medication?

4. How do you deal with the problem of side effects?

Session 5

During this session, we will be looking at the following frequently asked questions regarding treatment of schizophrenia

1. Can schizophrenia be treated?

2. How does medication help?

3. What are the side effects of my medication?

4. What will happen if I use alcohol or illegal drugs while on medication?

5. Can I smoke tobacco or drink caffeine?

6. What might happen if I experience any disturbing psychotic symptoms?

7. Why is it so important to keep taking my medication?

Session 5

▶ CAN SCHIZOPHRENIA BE TREATED?

There is not as yet a cure for schizophrenia.

But modern forms of drug treatment can control disturbing symptoms and reduce the effects that schizophrenia can have on your life.

Your medication can also help you to feel less anxious and also reduces the risk of a relapse by a half, which would reduce the chance of admission into hospital.

Antipsychotic medication plays a very important part and is currently the best treatment that is available, but this medication does not cure schizophrenia as stated above, nor does it guarantee that there will be no further psychotic episodes, but concentrates on treating the symptoms of schizophrenia.

What medication are you taking?

. . . .

. . . .

. . . .

. . . .

. . . .

As with all medication, however, people can experience unpleasant side effects, but they differ from one person to another. This will be discussed later in this session.

Because of the risk of relapses, it is usually wise to take medication for years, if not for life, much like a diabetic needs to continue taking insulin for the rest of their lives.

How do you feel about this?

. . . .

. . . .

. . . .

. . . .

. . . .

Sufferers should work in partnership with their doctor to find the right medication that best controls their symptoms with the fewest side effects.

There are some **psychological treatments** that also help, and these are Cognitive Behavioural Therapy (CBT) and family work. When these are used alongside medication treatment, they can help reduce the number of relapses you have. At the moment, they are not widely available, but this could change in the future. CBT is useful when you have troublesome symptoms, and family work helps by ensuring that family members understand your illness and its treatment.

Speak to your doctor as he or she may be able to refer you to a psychologist. Otherwise, there is a useful contact number at the end of this workbook if you would like to pursue this form of treatment.

Although talking treatments do not stop relapses or change symptoms, they give you the opportunity to spend time exploring your thoughts and feelings regarding your illness.

▶ HOW DOES MEDICATION HELP?

Antipsychotic medication works by blocking receptors; these are nerve cells in the brain which receive information. As already mentioned, it is believed that those who suffer from schizophrenia produce too much dopamine in the brain, and this antipsychotic medication affects a particular type of receptor that prevents a nerve cell from being stimulated and producing more dopamine.

Antipsychotic medication is divided into two types: **typical** and **atypical**.

A **typical** (conventional) antipsychotic medication is the older type of medication that is currently available and was first developed in the 1950s. As mentioned above, it works by reducing the action of a particular messenger in the brain called **dopamine**. This medication works on the positive symptoms of the illness.

The following are typical antipsychotic medications:

- chlorpromazine
- trifluoperazine
- haloperidol
- fluphenthixol

Atypical (newer) antipsychotic medication that has been developed over the past 10 years works on both the negative and positive symptoms of the illness and reduces the actions of both **dopamine** (transmitter of nerve impulses) and **serotonin** (mood regulator) in the brain.

Atypical antipsychotic medication includes:

- amisulpride
- olanzapine
- risperidone
- quetiapine
- aripiprazole
- clozapine

Have you been prescribed medication and, if so, was it atypical or typical?

．．

．．

．．

．．

Are you currently suffering from any side effects from your medication?

．．

．．

．．

．．

．．

Do you know your rights regarding taking your medication?

．．

．．

．．

．．

If not, speak to your doctor or keyworker.

Have you ever stopped taking your medication?

．．

Why?

．．

．．

．．

．．

．．

．．

Medication is usually given as a tablet, capsule, liquid or injection.

Do you prefer tablets or injections? Why?

．．

．．

．．

．．

．．

．．

DEPOT INJECTIONS

Many people have injections instead of taking tablets. These are called 'depot injections', which is a special preparation in a solution that is injected into the muscle.

Are you prescribed a depot?

. . . .

Antipsychotic depots include:

- Clopixol (zuclopenthixol decanoate)
- Depixol (flupenthixol decanoate)
- Risperidone (Risperdal Consta)

If you are having a depot, which one have you been prescribed and what dosage?

. . . .

. . . .

. . . .

Following an injection into the muscle, the medicine is slowly released into the blood-stream. This results in the medicine staying in the blood stream over fairly long periods, so that injections can be given every few weeks. Both tablets and injections help to reduce your symptoms and prevent them from returning.

When in the community, your depot will be given to you by a nurse in a clinic or a nurse can visit you in your home.

How do you feel about having your depot injections?

. . . .

. . . .

. . . .

. . . .

. . . .

▶ WHAT ARE THE SIDE EFFECTS OF MY MEDICATION?

Medication can help you to control the symptoms of your illness and enable you to return to a more normal life; however, there are side effects.

Have you experienced any side effects due to your medication?

. . . .

If so, what have you experienced?

. . . .

. . . .

. . . .

. . . .

How have you coped with these side effects?

. . . .

. . . .

. . . .

. . . .

All medication has side effects, including your antipsychotic medication that actually has some side effects which are helpful (for example they help you to feel less anxious or help you to sleep). But there are some side effects that are not helpful.

Some unhelpful side effects might be:

- stiffness
- dry mouth
- shaking and trembling
- constipation
- drowsiness
- sun sensitivity
- blurred vision
- hypersalivation
- amenorrhoea (absence of menstruation)
- sexual dysfunction
- weight gain.

Which side effects have you experienced?

. . . .

. . . .

. . . .

. . . .

You might get some side effects after taking your antipsychotic medication. The following pages will give you some advice on what to do if you get any of them. It's important to note that not everybody will experience these side effects shown (Mind, 2004).

Have you suffered from drowsiness as a side effect of your medication?

. . . .

Drowsiness

This is feeling a bit sluggish, which is a common side effect; the sedative's effects may be beneficial, though, to some people who feel agitated. However, this drowsiness tends to decrease after time. If this is a problem for you, speak to your doctor to see whether you can take medication at a different time, i.e. before going to bed.

Have you suffered from weight gain as a side effect of your medication?

. . . .

Weight gain

Some people find that the medication they are taking can lead to an increase in their appetite, which leads to weight gain.

If you are putting on too much weight:

- **look at what you are eating** – are you eating too much food or sugary drinks?
- **keep a diet diary** and note down *everything* you eat every day
- **look at when you eat** – try to eat at regular meal times and avoid eating before you go to bed
- **look at how much you eat** – avoid snacks and eat healthy, balanced meals
- **look at taking up some form of exercise** – just 30 minutes' walking a day would help.
- **drink more liquid** – we often mistake hunger for thirst (two litres a day is a recommended amount)

Consider speaking to your keyworker or doctor, or even consulting a qualified dietician, about a healthy, balanced diet.

EXTRAPYRAMIDAL SIDE EFFECTS

The following three symptoms are known as 'extrapyramidal side effects', or **EPS**. These vary in severity, and some people do not experience them at all. The final EPS mentioned on this page is a rare EPS that needs to be mentioned, but don't be alarmed as this is less common with the newer atypical medications.

Restlessness (or akathisia)

Akathisia is a feeling of inner restlessness and unease and causes you to want to pace up and down. This is a common side effect in the older medication but happens less often with some of the newer atypical medication. Restlessness responds well to dose reduction and also treatment with propranolol and sometimes procyclidine or orphenadrine.

Have you ever suffered from restlessness as a side effect of your medication?

. . . .

> ### Movement disorders (or Parkinsonism symptoms)
> Muscle stiffness, tremor or cramp are common side effects and are caused by changes in the brain as a result of your antipsychotic medication blocking dopamine receptors. When dopamine is reduced another chemical, acetylcholine, is increased; this causes your stiffness. This side effect can be reduced by taking procyclidine or orphenadrine, which reduce the action of acetylcholine.

Have you ever suffered from problems with your movement as a side effect of your medication?

. . . .

> ### Tardive dyskinesia
> This is a rare side effect and is the development of uncontrollable movements, usually of the face, lips and tongue. It affects up to 20% of sufferers on typical medication, but fortunately much progress has been made and the improved newer atypical medication has a much lower risk of producing these symptoms.

Have you ever suffered from uncontrollable movements as a side effect of your medication?

. . . .

Atypical medications are less likely to cause EPS side effects.

ANTICHOLINERGIC SIDE EFFECTS

The following side effects are known as 'anticholinergic side effects':

> ### Constipation
> Constipation means that you find it difficult to pass stools. It is a common side effect; eating more fibre and fruit, drink plenty of fluids and doing more exercise will help. You could also ask your doctor for a mild laxative.

Have you suffered from constipation as a side effect of your medication?

. . . .

> ### Blurred vision
> This means that things look blurry and you can't focus properly. This is not a common side effect; you must not drive. Speak to your doctor if you are worried.

Have you suffered from blurred vision as a side effect of your medication?

. . . .

> ### Hypotension
> Hypotension is low blood pressure, which can make you feel dizzy. This is common side effect. It will help if you try not to stand up too quickly.

Have you suffered from hypotension as a side effect of your medication?

. . . .

OTHER SIDE EFFECTS

| **Headaches** |
| This is a common side effect. Taking paracetamol will help. |

Have you suffered from headaches as a side effect of your medication?

. . . .

| **Skin rashes** |
| This means having blotches. This is not a common side effect. If it occurs, you must stop taking your medication and see your doctor immediately. |

Have you ever suffered from skin rashes as a side effect of your medication?

. . . .

| **Palpitations (or arrhythmia)** |
| A fast heart beat, or palpitations, are not a common side effect and can be easily treated if this lasts for a long time. |

Have you ever suffered from palpitations as a side effect of your medication?

. . . .

| **Impaired glucose tolerance** |
| This is not a common side effect and causes thirst, weakness and an excessive need to urinate. If you develop these symptoms, contact your doctor (Taylor *et al.*, 2005). |

Have you ever suffered from impaired glucose tolerance as a side effect of your medication?

. . . .

| **Amenorrhea (absence of periods)** |
| Raised prolactin caused by antipsychotic medication can affect periods in women. It is not common. You need to discuss this side effect with your doctor. The new atypical medications are less likely to cause these problems. |

Have you ever suffered from absence of periods (if you are a female)?

. . . .

> **Sexual dysfunction**
>
> This may cause sexual difficulties in men, and might cause them some distress, especially if they are in a relationship. It is important to remember that some sexual problems are very common amongst men that are not taking medication, i.e. stress, anxiety and alcohol.
>
> Because of these factors, it makes it difficult to assess whether sexual problems are directly due to psychiatric medication alone. There are other medications that have been known to cause sexual problems. These are blood pressure, antidepressants and indigestion medication. You need to speak to your doctor, who may adjust your dosage or change your medication.

Have you suffered from difficulties in sexual dysfunction?

. . . .

Have you understood all of these side effects (pages 60–64)? If you're still not sure, go through them again with your keyworker as it is important that you understand how your medication affects you so that you understand what causes the side effects and what can help you to deal with these problems.

CLOZAPINE

If you are prescribed clozapine medication, the following information will be useful to you. If you are not, move on to page 66.

Clozapine is an atypical antipsychotic and is often more effective than other antipsychotic medication, but it is not suitable for everybody. This is because it can cause a problem with the white blood cells (agranulocytosis) of some people, and therefore regular blood tests need to be taken when clozapine is prescribed.

Agranulocytosis is a condition whereby your white blood cells are low. White blood cells fight infection. If you have too few white blood cells, it will be harder for you to fight off infection. A weekly blood test will make sure that your white blood cells are at a safe level. After 18 weeks you should only need a blood test every fortnight and, after a year, you will only need to have a blood test every four weeks.

A **blood-monitoring service** is available when clozapine is prescribed and will inform your doctor regarding your blood test. The reading of your blood test will be either a green, amber or red result:

- Green means that it is safe to continue taking your clozapine medication.
- Amber means that it is safe to continue taking your medication, but you will be monitored very closely by the blood monitoring service and your doctor.
- Red means your doctor will advise you to stop taking your medication.

It is very important that you have a blood test because *no* tablets can be given out until the blood monitoring service has checked that it is safe for you to continue.

Inform your doctor if you develop any infections like a sore throat or flu-like symptoms.

THE SIDE EFFECTS OF TAKING CLOZAPINE

Alongside some of the side effects discussed above, clozapine also has five other possible side effects.

Orthostatic hypotension

This is a common side effect. It causes your blood pressure to become low making you feel dizzy when you stand up too quickly. Try to stand up slowly from a sitting position.

Hypersalivation

Your pillow may be wet when you wake up in the morning. If it annoys you, your doctor can prescribe a tablet (hyoscine or procyclidine) that will help.

Agranulocytosis (or Neutropenia)

This is not a common side effect and is when there is a low number of white blood cells in your blood. Hence you may get more infections. This will be picked up in your regular blood tests. But you must always tell your doctor or nurse if you feel ill in any way (e.g. sore throat).

Seizures

This is not a common side effect and is when some people have a fit. If this happens to you, stop taking clozapine and contact your doctor immediately.

Fever

This side effect is rare; so you must speak to your doctor if you develop a high temperature.

(Lewis *et al.*, 2006)

To help cope with any of the side effects due to any of the antipsychotic medication discussed in this section, your doctor may be able to:

- reduce the dosage of your medication to lessen the side effects
- change your medication for another
- prescribe another drug to counteract them, such as procyclidine or orphenadrine.

The choice is not an easy one and needs the understanding of everyone concerned.

REDUCING THE SIDE EFFECTS OF MEDICATION

It has to be said that some of the side effects can be reduced by taking **procyclidine** or **orphenadrine**, which work by reducing the action of acetylcholine. However, as already stated, most drugs have side effects and these drugs are no exception (their side effects are a dryness of mouth and constipation). But these are easier to cope with than perhaps stiffness, which the antipsychotic drugs cause.

Have you needed to ever take procyclidine or orphenadrine to help with the side effects of your medication? Did it help?

. . . .

Sucking a sweet or drinking regularly may help with a dry mouth. Eating more fibre (fruit and vegetables) may help with constipation.

Would you like to discuss your current medication with your doctor?

. . . .

If so, why?

. . . .

. . . .

. . . .

If you developed side effects, would you discuss these with your doctor?

. . . .

If you wouldn't, could your keyworker help you to approach your doctor?

. . . .

▶ WHAT HAPPENS IF I STOP TAKING MY MEDICATION?

As mentioned before, like diabetes or high blood pressure, schizophrenia is a chronic illness that needs constant management. **Relapses occur most often when people stop taking their medication** because they:

- feel better and don't think they need it
- forget to take it or take it occasionally
- don't think medication is important
- suffer from unpleasant side effects
- believe that medication only needs to be taken when they are feeling unwell
- challenge the diagnosis of schizophrenia and so contend that they don't need medication.

Have you ever stopped taking your medication in the past?

. . . .

If so, why you did stop taking your medication?

. . . .

. . . .

. . . .

Have you ever forgotten to take your medication?

. . . .

If so, how can you ensure that you don't forget to take your medication in the future?

. . . .

. . . .

Have you ever relapsed in your illness because you did not take your medication?

. . . .

Do you think you will continue taking your medication once discharged?

. . . .

Why?

. . . .

. . . .

. . . .

. . . .

. . . .

It is very important that you take your medication on a regular basis and for as long as the doctor recommends. If you do so, you will experience fewer psychotic symptoms.

If you are suffering from any side effects and they are becoming upsetting and distressing for you, talk to your doctor or keyworker, who will attempt to address your problems.

Some people will develop tolerance to some of these side effects. But if they are persistent and are affecting the quality of your life, you need to speak to your doctor to change to a drug that will work better for you.

> **Do not stop your medication or cut it down by yourself.**

MEDICATION: THE BENEFITS

What are the benefits of continuing to take your medication?

. . . .

. . . .

. . . .

. . . .

. . . .

. . . .

. . . .

The most important benefit of taking medication is that it will help you to control the symptoms of your illness, and for this reason is a step closer to rebuilding your life.

Finding the right medication and dosage to suit you is, however, not that easy. Discovering the most effective treatment with the fewest side effects can take time and demands patience and understanding from all of the parties concerned – from the doctor and the keyworker to the sufferer and their family.

To recap, what *can* medication do for you?

. . . .

. . . .

. . . .

. . . .

It can cut down the risk of a relapse in your illness, reduce your negative and positive symptoms and lower your anxiety. Medication can also help you to think more clearly and to feel better in yourself. It also increases your motivation to look after yourself.

What can medication *not* do for you?

. . . .

. . . .

. . . .

. . . .

It cannot always prevent a relapse, and nor can it always put a stop to your symptoms. Above all, it cannot cure schizophrenia.

Has there been a time when you were 'reasonably well' and 'on' medication? How did you feel?

. . . .

. . . .

. . . .

. . . .

. . . .

. . . .

. . . .

Has there been a time when you were 'unwell' and 'off' medication? How did you feel?

. . . .

. . . .

. . . .

. . . .

. . . .

. . . .

. . . .

$$\boxed{\text{It's really all up to you!}}$$

If you stop taking your tablets and injections, the symptoms of schizophrenia will usually come back, not immediately, but usually within six months.

Is it worth risking your mental health by stopping your medication, without the advice from your doctor?

. . . .

▶ WHAT WILL HAPPEN IF I USE ALCOHOL OR ILLEGAL DRUGS WHILE ON MEDICATION?

Illegal drugs or alcohol do *not* go together with antipsychotic medication and are definitely *not* a good combination. The results are that when more than one drug is taken at the same time one drug may be changed by the presence of the other, such as one drug becoming toxic or the level of your medication's effectiveness being lowered.

This can make your symptoms worse and cause you to relapse in your illness.

Did you ever use illegal drugs or alcohol as a form of self-medication to help with your symptoms?

. . . .

If so, how did taking illegal drugs or alcohol help?

. . . .

. . . .

. . . .

Have you ever taken illegal drugs or alcohol while on medication?

. . . .

If so, what did you experience?

. . . .

. . . .

. . . .

. . . .

If you take illegal drugs while on medication, this might trigger your symptoms to return, causing you to be distressed by your symptoms and will set you back for a long time.

Is it worth it?

. . . .

Endorphins are naturally occurring neurotransmitters (special chemicals in the brain) that relieve pain and increase pleasure. Some illegal drugs mimic (copy) endorphins, thus causing the same effect. There are some safe ways to achieve a *natural* high (that is without taking illegal drugs) and this is by doing some form of exercise.

Alcohol is not recommended with antipsychotic medication as it causes drowsiness, but with guidance from your doctor you may be able to drink alcohol in moderation.

Do you need help in alcohol/illegal drug counselling?

. . . .

If so, speak to your doctor or keyworker.

▶ CAN I SMOKE TOBACCO OR DRINK CAFFEINE?

How many cigarettes do you smoke a day?

. . . .

There has been some research that states that if you smoke cigarettes you will need to be on a higher dose of antipsychotic medication. This is because smoking increases the breakdown of the medication quicker so you will need more medication for it to have any effect on you. If you are thinking about stopping or cutting down on your tobacco intake, inform your doctor (Goff *et al.*, 1992).

How much coffee, tea, Red Bull or Coca Cola do you drink a day?

. . . .

There has also been some strong evidence that excessive caffeine intake can increase your psychotic symptoms and the side effects of your medication. Think about decaffeinated drinks (Winston *et al.*, 2005).

▶ WHAT MIGHT HAPPEN IF I EXPERIENCE ANY DISTURBING PSYCHOTIC SYMPTOMS?

When experiencing any disturbing symptoms of psychosis, you can become more vulnerable to yourself and to others:

RISK TO YOURSELF

Neglecting your basic self-care

When unwell, have you not bothered to look after yourself and have your relatives been concerned about you neglecting yourself? If so, list examples of when you were unwell and how you neglected yourself.

. . . .

. . . .

. . . .

. . . .

Causing harm to yourself

When unwell, did you have thoughts of harming yourself? If so, can you give any examples of when you harmed yourself?

. . . .

. . . .

. . . .

. . . .

Risk of being exploited by others

When unwell, were you used by others for their own benefit? If so, give examples of when this happened.

. . . .

. . . .

. . . .

. . . .

RISK TO OTHERS

Harm to others

When unwell, have you been a risk to others or committed a crime? If so, can you give any examples of this?

. . . .

. . . .

. . . .

. . . .

ADMISSION INTO HOSPITAL

If you become unwell or relapse, you may want to go somewhere where you will feel safe. This might be a hospital, and if you voluntarily agree to an informal admission for treatment you are free to leave hospital whenever you wish.

If you were very unwell and were out of touch with reality (that is you could not separate what was real from what was not real) because of your upsetting symptoms, you would not realise that you were ill and may refuse to be admitted to hospital.

Has this ever happened to you?

. . . .

. . . .

. . . .

You may refuse treatment when you really need it, and so if you are unwilling to admit yourself to hospital, to protect you from harming yourself or other people, you can be compulsorily admitted under the provisions of the Mental Health Act (1983). This is only used by health or social services if someone needs assessment or treatment but will not accept this.

If this did happen to you, how did you feel at the time?

. . . .

. . . .

. . . .

If you are kept in hospital under this law, you can appeal against the decision. You will be told this when you are admitted into hospital.

Once you have been sectioned or detained in hospital, you may be subject to a **supervised discharge**. This means your care will be supervised after you leave hospital (Mind, 2006).

Do you remember your mental state when you were first admitted to hospital? Can you describe it now?

. . . .

. . . .

. . . .

. . . .

. . . .

. . . .

. . . .

. . . .

. . . .

. . . .

. . . .

. . . .

▶ WHY IS IT SO IMPORTANT TO KEEP TAKING MY MEDICATION?

What has helped you achieve the mental state you have at present?

. . . .

. . . .

. . . .

. . . .

. . . .

. . . .

. . . .

What could change this?

. . . .

. . . .

. . . .

. . . .

. . . .

. . . .

. . . .

Do you think you need to continue taking medication? Why?

. . . .

. . . .

. . . .

. . . .

. . . .

. . . .

. . . .

The symptoms of schizophrenia often come back. This is much less likely to happen if you continue to take your medication, even if you feel well. This is why doctors suggest that you take this medication for a long time.

If you stopped taking your medication now, without the advice of doctors and nurses, and your distressing symptoms returned, what risk would this pose to your own mental health and also the safety of yourself and others?

. . . .

. . . .

. . . .

. . . .

. . . .

Isn't it worth taking your medication?

. . . .

. . . .

. . . .

. . . .

So, to recap, what are the benefits for you if you continue to take your medication?

. . . .

. . . .

. . . .

. . . .

. . . .

. . . .

. . . .

. . . .

. . . .

. . . .

. . . .

. . . .

. . . .

. . . .

. . . .

Researchers stated in 2003 that they saw 'a cure for schizophrenia as possible in 10 years'. This is by decoding the human genome (genetics) and by the better targeting of medication for schizophrenia with fewer side effects (National Alliance for the Mentally Ill, 2003).

While this means that much more money will have to be put into research, there is hope for the future.

> **Remember, at present, schizophrenia cannot be cured but it can be treated.**

▶ **End-of-session Questionnaire**

What three important things have you learnt and will take away with you from Session 5 (you may need to browse through the session again to jog your memory)?

1) ....
....
....
....
....
....
....
....
....
....

2) ....
....
....
....
....
....
....
....
....

3) ....
....
....
....
....
....
....
....
....

Session 6

▶ Questionnaire

These questions are not meant to be seen as a test. They are only a means of sharing information and getting you to think about your illness before you start your session. If you're not sure, just make a guess: there are no right or wrong answers.

1. What symptoms do you think you would experience if you became unwell again?

2. What plans do you have for the future?

Session 6

During this session, we will be looking at the following frequently asked questions regarding the treatment of schizophrenia:

1. What can I do to keep myself well?

2. What are the early-warning signs of a relapse in my illness?

3. How do I prevent a relapse?

4. How can I cope with my 'voices'?

5. What can I do to deal with my strange ideas?

6. How can I improve my confidence and rebuild my life?

7. What effect will my illness have on my relationships with my family and friends?

▶ WHAT CAN I DO TO KEEP MYSELF WELL?

In this session we will be looking at some practical ideas on how to keep well. There will also be some useful ideas on how to control and cope with your symptoms. Furthermore, there will be advice on what to do if you feel you are getting unwell again.

Before we continue this session, we need to explore whether you feel in a challenging mood or not.

Because you have schizophrenia, it does not mean you cannot have a normal life like those who do not suffer from schizophrenia. The symptoms that you suffer from are not considered 'normal', but you can have successful lives like others and as already discussed regarding famous people with schizophrenia (page 36). They have managed to have successful occupations, happy family lives and make a contribution to society. You don't have to be famous to achieve the above; you can be just you, and happen to suffer from schizophrenia.

Some of you may not be ready to see this illness as a challenge and may want to be seen as a victim of your diagnosis, wanting others to rally around for you. If this is the stage that you are at, then that is fine. Nearly all illnesses, physical and psychological, make us feel like this at some stage, making us think:

- 'What's the point?'
- 'Nothing will change.'
- 'It sounds like hard work and I don't have the energy.'

But eventually there will be a time where you want something different and you will want to live your life with more hope and passion.

The key is *you* taking control of your illness and *not* letting your illness control you. You can do so much to keep yourself well. In this session we will explore:

- learning how to cope with 'voices'
- learning how to cope with strange ideas
- learning about the early-warning signs of your illness returning
- learning how to improve your confidence and rebuild your life
- looking at family relationships
- looking at intimate relationships
- how to be assertive.

> **Do you want to take up the challenge?**

▶ WHAT ARE THE EARLY-WARNING SIGNS OF A RELAPSE IN MY ILLNESS?

Most people with schizophrenia have been through a psychotic episode and, although you would prefer to forget this and hope that it won't happen again, you must develop skills that will help you to reduce or prevent another relapse in the future.

From time to time, your psychosis may show signs of coming back and these early symptoms are called your 'early-warning signs', which can take up to a month to develop.

This part of the session is aimed at helping you to identify your personal early-warning signs (or **relapse signature**), which is essential if you want to prevent yourself from having a relapse. Also this is powerful information because it is the way forward for you to gaining some control over your illness.

How does this make you feel, thinking that perhaps you may have some control over your illness?

. . . .

. . . .

. . . .

. . . .

What is hoped during this session is for you to devise two relapse-prevention action plans, which are called a 'relapse drill' and 'advanced directive', which will be helpful information for you, your family and professionals if you become unwell again in the future.

These signs below are warnings to you that a relapse may be coming on.

Some possible warnings signs are:

1. **Changes in the way you think**
That is the ideas and beliefs you had about yourself or others, for example you may become suspicious of others' intentions.
2. **Changes in your behaviour**
That is changes in your relationship with others, your eating or sleep pattern and doing unusual things, for example wanting to stay in bed a lot
3. **Changes in the way you feel**
You feel more anxious or sensitive towards others or your mood is changeable, for example feeling low.

Think back to the time you were unwell, how did you feel in the few weeks beforehand?

. . . .

. . . .

. . . .

. . . .

Below are some common early-warning signs; identify the ones that you have experienced:

You may need to really think about this one, or ask a member of your family or mental health worker who knows you well who may be able to remember things you have forgotten. Tick either the 'Yes' or 'No' box.

Changes in my thinking

My 'voices' return or worsen	Yes ☐ No ☐
I find it hard to concentrate	Yes ☐ No ☐
I think that I am being watched	Yes ☐ No ☐
I think that my thoughts might be controlled	Yes ☐ No ☐
I have thoughts of hurting or killing myself	Yes ☐ No ☐
My thoughts are so fast, I can't keep up with them	Yes ☐ No ☐
New ideas are constantly coming into my head	Yes ☐ No ☐
I think I have special powers	Yes ☐ No ☐
I get bothered by thoughts I cannot get rid of	Yes ☐ No ☐
I have thoughts of hurting others	Yes ☐ No ☐
I am preoccupied with sexual thoughts	Yes ☐ No ☐
I receive messages from the TV/radio	Yes ☐ No ☐
I have trouble making everyday decisions	Yes ☐ No ☐
I am preoccupied with disturbing thoughts	Yes ☐ No ☐
I think that others don't care about me	Yes ☐ No ☐
I think that others are trying to hurt me or make me ill	Yes ☐ No ☐
I think I am going 'mad'	Yes ☐ No ☐
I think people are making fun of me or that they are laughing or talking about me	Yes ☐ No ☐

List all the early-warning signs that you have experienced above and **remember this as your signature relapse**. This is very helpful to you because it relates to the changes in your thinking. If you experienced them again in the future, it should indicate to you that possibly you may be relapsing and that you need to seek help quickly.

1. ....

2. ....

3. ....

4. ....

5. ....

Include other symptoms not mentioned here:

....

....

Changes in my behaviour

I have the urge to spend a lot of money	Yes ☐ No ☐
I talk more than usual	Yes ☐ No ☐
I smoke more	Yes ☐ No ☐
My sleep is restless or unsettled	Yes ☐ No ☐
I behave oddly for no reason	Yes ☐ No ☐
I have no appetite	Yes ☐ No ☐
I feel violent and aggressive	Yes ☐ No ☐
I talk to myself	Yes ☐ No ☐
I don't bother to wash or care about myself	Yes ☐ No ☐
I lose my temper easily	Yes ☐ No ☐
I feel tired and lethargic	Yes ☐ No ☐
I behave like I have no respect for authority	Yes ☐ No ☐
I talk in ways that don't make sense to others	Yes ☐ No ☐
I have bad dreams	Yes ☐ No ☐
Religion becomes more meaningful	Yes ☐ No ☐
I shave my head or body hair	Yes ☐ No ☐
I use strange words others don't understand	Yes ☐ No ☐
I smile to myself	Yes ☐ No ☐
I don't go to my activities or groups	Yes ☐ No ☐
I go on long walks leading nowhere in particular	Yes ☐ No ☐
I act suspiciously like I am being watched	Yes ☐ No ☐
I write things down all the time	Yes ☐ No ☐
I lose weight	Yes ☐ No ☐
I gain weight	Yes ☐ No ☐
Others tell me that I am acting differently	Yes ☐ No ☐
I stay in bed more than usual	Yes ☐ No ☐
I am sensitive to noise or lights	Yes ☐ No ☐
I isolate myself and act like a recluse	Yes ☐ No ☐
I get into a lot of arguments	Yes ☐ No ☐
I don't bother to see my friends	Yes ☐ No ☐
I say things that seem deep to me but illogical to others	Yes ☐ No ☐
I use illegal drugs or alcohol to deal with my experience	Yes ☐ No ☐
My family and friends tell me that 'I am not the same'	Yes ☐ No ☐

List all of the early-warning signs that you have experienced above, and remember this as your **signature relapse**.

1. . . . .

2. . . . .

3. . . . .

4. . . . .

5. . . . .

Include other symptoms not mentioned here:

. . . .

. . . .

Changes in my feelings

I feel depressed or low in my mood	Yes ☐ No ☐
I feel helpless and useless	Yes ☐ No ☐
I feel irritable	Yes ☐ No ☐
I feel tense or anxious	Yes ☐ No ☐
I feel like I am being watched	Yes ☐ No ☐
I feel strong and powerful	Yes ☐ No ☐
I feel I am being punished	Yes ☐ No ☐
I feel very excited	Yes ☐ No ☐
I feel forgetful	Yes ☐ No ☐
I feel unable to cope with everyday things	Yes ☐ No ☐
I feel quiet and withdrawn	Yes ☐ No ☐
I feel I can't trust anyone	Yes ☐ No ☐
I am unable to express my emotions	Yes ☐ No ☐
I feel my surroundings are strange	Yes ☐ No ☐
I feel bad for no reason	Yes ☐ No ☐
I feel like I am in another world	Yes ☐ No ☐

List all of the early-warning signs that you have experienced above, and remember this as your **signature relapse**.

1. . . . .

2. . . . .

3. . . . .

4. . . . .

5. . . . .

Include other symptoms not mentioned here:

. . . .

. . . .

. . . .

. . . .

. . . .

. . . .

. . . .

. . . .

You may need to write on another piece of paper if necessary.

A practical exercise: write on some flash cards the early-warning signs you have identified and try to make them more personal to you, for example, 'I hear a male voice that is critical and nasty to me', 'I don't wash for two weeks' or 'I don't have a shower for weeks on end'. Next, lay the cards on a table and put them in the order in which they happened, for example the **first changes** you noticed, such as difficulty sleeping, to the **last changes** you noticed, such as hearing voices, and note these down as part of your **relapse signature** (Smith, 2005).

FALSE ALARMS

> **It is important to remember that if your psychosis is returning you will feel a significant change in the way that you feel and think about things.**

There are always going to be times when we all feel nervous or don't feel like talking to people, but if these are only for a short period then its doubtful that they are actual early-warning signs.

You will know if these are definitely your early-warning signs because they will get worse and you will become more aware of them as time goes by.

TRIGGER EVENTS

The next issues you need to identify are the situations that might trigger your psychosis. For some people, situations like starting college, moving house, starting a new job, physical illness, relationship breakdowns with family/friends/partners or a bereavement may cause a relapse in their illness because of the stress that they are experiencing.

You need to be aware of situations that make you prone to stress.

Looking back to when you were unwell, were there any stressful situations that might have set off your psychosis? Can you describe it/them?

. . . .

. . . .

. . . .

. . . .

. . . .

Stress is a part of our everyday life. It is going to be hard to totally avoid every stressful situation. But what you could do is anticipate certain situations and make a plan on how to deal with them. You can also learn strategies on how to cope better with stress, as discussed in Session 2.

Over the page is a contract (advanced directive) that would be helpful for you to complete and identifies your relapse signature and alerts others to your situation. This is most helpful when you have lost insight into your illness and helps those who care about you to take action with your permission.

Advanced Directive

I . . . . .have a relapse signature which is:

- Changes in my thinking . . . .
. . . .
. . . .
. . . .
. . . .

- Changes in my behaviour . . . .
. . . .
. . . .
. . . .
. . . .

- Changes in my feelings . . . .
. . . .
. . . .
. . . .
. . . .

- When unwell, I am particularly at high risk when . . . .
. . . .
. . . .
. . . .
. . . .

- The following treatments have been helpful to me in the past
. . . .
. . . .
. . . .
. . . .

- People I need to inform when my symptoms return are:
. . . . .telephone number . . . .
. . . . .telephone number . . . .
. . . . .telephone number . . . .

I am asking the people above to help me to be aware of my own early-warning signs and bring them to my attention. If any of the above are my family and I refuse to seek any help, I am in agreement for them to contact my doctor.

Signed . . . . Date . . . .

(Photocopy this and give a copy to your family and doctor)

Understanding Your Schizophrenia Illness: A Workbook, Chris Healy,
© 2007 by John Wiley & Sons, Ltd.

Even though these changes happen over a matter of weeks, you will notice a definite change in your mental state. However, now that you have identified your early-warning signs, what can you do if you notice them coming back?

▶ HOW DO I PREVENT A RELAPSE?

Once you have identified your relapse signature, you need to work out what to do when your early-warning signs return. This is called a 'relapse drill' (Birchwood *et al.*, 2000).

First, you must keep calm and in control, plus you must contact your doctor or mental health worker straight away. As already mentioned they may suggest that you increase your medication for a short time to help stop the psychosis returning. Also you need to put into practice ways of handling stress (see Session 2, pages 20–24).

See page 87 for your relapse drill.

Relapse Drill

Step 1

Stay calm by using relaxation techniques (write them down)

. . . .

. . . .

. . . .

Contact . . . . for support family/friend

Contact . . . . for support health professional

Step 2

What distraction or coping techniques would help you?

. . . .

. . . .

. . . .

. . . .

. . . .

. . . .

Contact doctor/community nurse regarding reviewing your medication

Dr/CPN . . . . .telephone number . . . .

Step 3

Consider informal or voluntary admission into hospital for assessment or treatment if this is what health professionals are suggesting.

(Photocopy this and give a copy to your family and professionals)

Understanding Your Schizophrenia Illness: A Workbook, Chris Healy,
© 2007 by John Wiley & Sons, Ltd.

It is very important that you seek help straight away because once the psychosis develops the symptoms of the illness will be obvious to those around you but not always to yourself, because after a while you will start to lose touch with reality.

To start with, you become very certain that your problems are not caused by your illness, and since you are not able to recognise what is happening you will become very vulnerable and, as a consequence, will become a risk to yourself and others. The world around you will seem very confusing to you and you will act and say things in a way that makes little sense to others.

It is hoped that through these sessions you will have gained some knowledge and awareness of how your illness affects you so that you can recognise when you are becoming unwell.

Looking back over the history of your illness, can you remember a situation when it seemed that you had lacked insight into your illness?

When? . . . .

Where? . . . .

What happened? . . . .

. . . .

. . . .

. . . .

If it ever happens again, do you know what you are going to do the next time?

. . . .

. . . .

However, try not to be too anxious about your psychosis returning because if you have prepared yourself you will be the one who is in control of your illness.

▶ HOW CAN I COPE WITH MY 'VOICES'?

Coping with your 'voices' is not only about reducing the experience of them, but also reducing the power they have over you.

Some sufferers may only experience 'voices' during an acute phase of their illness, and sometimes sufferers have residual symptoms, that is they experience 'voices' when appearing 'well' and there is no other symptom of psychosis evident.

Have you experienced 'voices' and what was the experience like for you?

. . . .

. . . .

. . . .

. . . .

. . . .

'Voices' have been described as a coping mechanism and that people generate their own voice as a means of coping with difficult feelings. Could your 'voices' be caused by any pressure or stress you may or might have been under?

What you need to remember is that these 'voices' are not real and that they come from your own mind.

The 'voices' may frighten you, because they may try to get you to do things that you don't want to do and you might feel compelled to do what they ask. That is the power that sometimes they can have over you. But you need to regain your power and not do what the 'voices' ask; however, this can be hard.

What you need to remember is that the 'voices' cannot harm you.

Although 'voices' in themselves cannot harm you, some sufferers may act out by carrying through the instructions given by the 'voices', and this may cause them harm.
If you have experienced 'voices', how have you tried to cope with them?

. . . .

. . . .

What worked the best?

. . . .

. . . .

. . . .

There are other ideas that might help you to cope with your 'voices', whether they are pleasant or unpleasant to you. You may want to include some of these activities and distractions in your **relapse drill**.

Try to keep as calm as possible.

Do some activities like:

- tidying the house
- having a relaxing bath
- walking
- going to the gym
- changing positions e.g. sit, stand, walk, run or lie down
- singing
- jogging
- mouth and jaw exercises
- taking extra medication
- using earplugs

- breathing exercises
- relaxation methods
- put fingers in your ears and close your eyes
- talk to a trusted friend or mental health worker
- ring someone on the telephone.

Do some distractions like:

- listening to music
- reading aloud
- watching TV or listening to the radio
- hobbies
- counting backwards from 100
- describing an object in detail
- writing a diary or poetry.

Do some interacting with the 'voices' like:

- agreeing to listen to the 'voices' at a particular time
- try not to argue with the 'voices', as they will get worse and upset you more
- don't do what the 'voices' ask, because if you do you may find it harder to stop, especially if they make you feel afraid.

'Voices' often tell lies and make false predictions.

Remember: it is you who makes the decisions, not your 'voices'.

▶ WHAT CAN I DO TO DEAL WITH MY STRANGE IDEAS?

You may suffer from worrying ideas or beliefs, which you feel really sure about but other people do not share.

These might be bad thoughts or feelings, and when you tell other people they will not agree with you. You may feel suspicious and paranoid of others and this could cause problems between you, your family and friends.

Have you ever felt that people are against you, or might wish you some harm?

. . . .

. . . .

Have you ever felt that you have special powers or that you can read people's thoughts?

. . . .

. . . .

Have you ever felt that your whole body and mind were under the control of some outside force?

. . . .

. . . .

Have you ever felt that people are talking about you on the radio or TV?

. . . .

. . . .

If you have experienced any of the above, you may have suffered from, or are currently suffering from, a delusion.

How does this make you feel?

. . . .

. . . .

These symptoms can be very distressing for you, but it is important that you try and stay calm during these times, or else you may make these ideas even stronger.

Delusions brought on by a psychotic episode may be perceived by the sufferer as religious experiences – that the 'voice' they hear is that of a god – and so they may begin to perceive the world and treat with it in purely religious terms. This can be more difficult for a sufferer who already has religious beliefs, which are then heightened by delusional ideas about divine 'voices', for example. The sufferer might need to attempt to understand what part their religious beliefs play in any psychotic episode. Pastoral support from your church or religious organisation might help you deal with the more extreme or worrying aspects of your religious delusions.

You also must try and not allow the ideas to affect your day-to-day living, and, although you might feel that the belief is very real, it is important for you to remember that no harm will come to you, because these ideas are part of your illness. So carry on as you would usually, for example by going to the shops or visiting your family.

It would help if you could keep your mind busy and away from these thoughts, but this is easier said than done. But keeping your mind busy helps, because it stops you from focusing too much on these beliefs, as this can lead to these beliefs taking over your life.

Things that you can do, for example, are listening to music, doing a hobby, exercising, watching TV, having a bath, reading a book or talking to a trusted friend. You could check out your beliefs and find out whether there is any evidence that would either confirm or dismiss them.

If you have experienced paranoia did you think you *knew exactly* what people were thinking (usually something negative about you)?

. . . .

Try not to read people's mind, because you will think your suspicions are a fact and will tell yourself that this is the proof. But how sure are you that you are right?

. . . .

Has people looking at you caused you to have paranoid thoughts?

. . . .

Try not to take this personally and think of other reasons why people might be looking at you, for example: 'They are looking at me because they like my shirt.'

Talk to someone about your fears so that you can have another viewpoint on the issue. Also think about the time when you looked or talked about someone else. If you did not mean them any harm then, maybe these people looking at you now don't either.

It has been said that sometimes delusions are a coping mechanism and that people hold onto their beliefs in order to protect their self-esteem.

It has been said that people suffering from paranoia often reject themselves and think that others will do the same (Chadwick *et al.*, 1996). Is this is how you feel about yourself?

. . . .

▶ HOW CAN I IMPROVE MY CONFIDENCE AND REBUILD MY LIFE?

This session is about improving your confidence and rebuilding your life, whether you are living in a hostel, flat or with your family.

If you have spent some time in hospital, you might find that your life has changed in many ways, for example you may not have a job, your interests and hobbies are not the same and you might not go out as much, because you may have lost contact with your friends.

This can make you feel fed up and will affect your confidence. If you have spent time in hospital, you can be sure that most people prior to their discharge and after discharge feel the same way. One of the common mistakes that most people make when they are in hospital is that they *only* concentrate on getting out of hospital. They don't think *beyond* their discharge, and this can, understandably, cause some anxiety.

Many people with your difficulties have found that with help they can begin to improve their lives by:

- mixing with people
- keeping themselves busy
- taking life steadily
- trying not to let others do too many things for them.

We will look at each of the these issues in more detail and suggest ideas on how you can balance your lifestyle and improve you quality of life, which would also reduce stress and tension in your life.

MIXING WITH PEOPLE

Go to day centres, social clubs or college classes, voluntary work and visit relatives. Below are suggestions of where you could mix with people. Tick one of the columns for each idea.

Activity	Not interested	Maybe interested	Yes interested
Go to a sporting event (e.g. football)			
Go to a day centre			
Meet a friend			
Join a self-help group			
Go to the cinema			
Go to dancing lessons			
Telephone friends, family or someone you have not spoken to for a while			
Learn to drive			
Do voluntary work			
Go to work			
Visit family			
Start evening or day courses			
Learn to play a musical instrument			

You need to think of as many places as possible of where you can mix with people. List what you are going to do below:

. . . .

. . . .

. . . .

. . . .

If you said *no* to some of the above suggestions, why did you?

. . . .

. . . .

If you said *maybe* to some of the suggestions, what is stopping you?

. . . .

. . . .

KEEP YOURSELF BUSY

Think about old hobbies or something you have always fancied doing. Below are suggestions for things you can do with your time. Tick one of the columns for each idea.

Activity	Not interested	Maybe interested	Yes interested
Go for a walk or join a gym			
Sit in the sun and relax			
Do some gardening			
Collect things (e.g. coins/stamps)			
Browse in antiques shops			
Learn a foreign language			
Paint a picture			
Join library and read a book			
Do arts and crafts			
Do needlework or knitting			
Listen to the radio and buy records/CDs			
Write a diary			
Play pool/snooker/darts			
Go to beach whatever the weather			
Visit places of interest			
Visit a car-boot sale			
Decorate room or do DIY			
Surf the Internet			
Watch TV or funny films			

Is there something else you would like to do or learn?

. . . .

. . . .

. . . .

. . . .

List what you are going to do with your time from the above list.

. . . .

. . . .

. . . .

. . . .

If you said *no* to any of the suggestions, why did you?

. . . .

. . . .

If you said *maybe* to any of the suggestions, what is stopping you?

. . . .

. . . .

. . . .

You might want to return to work or studies, and under the Disability Discrimination Act 1995 employers must provide 'reasonable adjustments' to facilitate the employment of disabled people, including those with mental health issues.

TAKE LIFE STEADILY

Don't put yourself under too much pressure. Find things that you can do easily and build up your confidence.

You may also need to look differently at how you solve problems, for example sorting out any financial issues. If you are having difficulties managing your money, you need to first work out how much you spend each week, for example on food and rent. Then work out the money you have coming in. Then, if you're spending more than your income, you will need to find ways of spending less money where possible. You can seek help from a social worker, the community psychiatric nurse (CPN) or the Citizens Advice Bureau.

How much is a:

small loaf of bread? . . . .

pint of milk? . . . .

small bottle of tomato sauce? . . . .

small jar of coffee? . . . .

packet of sugar? . . . .

toothbrush? . . . .

half a dozen eggs? . . . .

small box of cornflakes? . . . .

TRY NOT TO LET OTHERS DO TOO MANY THINGS FOR YOU

Do as much as you can for yourself, for example washing your clothes, shopping and cooking. See the table on page 96 for suggestions of what you should try to do for yourself. Tick one of the columns for each suggestion.

Activities	Not interested	Maybe interested	Yes interested
Wash, iron clothes			
Cook three meals a day			
Eat something you have never eaten before			
Learn new recipes			
Do food shopping			
Clean house/room			
Save money			
Go out on a date			
Go to hairdresser's/barber's or change hairstyle			
Take medication			
Learn more about your illness			
Go for a run			
Visit dentist			
If concerned about your weight, speak to someone about healthy eating or join a self-help group			
Look after a pet			
Sort out your wardrobe and buy new clothes			

List the meals you would like to learn how to cook

. . . .

. . . .

What domestic tasks do you feel you need help with?

. . . .

. . . .

Identify the three main pleasurable activities you intend to incorporate into your week

Activity 1

. . . .

. . . .

Activity 2

. . . .

. . . .

Activity 3

. . . .

. . . .

List three goals you would *really* like to achieve in your life.

1) . . . .

2) . . . .

3) . . . .

How do you think you could go about trying to achieve one of these goals?

. . . .

. . . .

. . . .

. . . .

. . . .

ASSERTIVENESS

Sometimes when people have developed a mental illness like schizophrenia it can take all of their confidence away. They might feel unable to stand up for their rights and prefer to be more passive in their dealings with others. This is understandable given how intense the illness can be.

What does 'assertiveness' mean to you?

. . . .

. . . .

. . . .

. . . .

Assertiveness is a skill that can be learnt and can help you to deal more effectively with difficult situations, which would help you in the long term to reduce your stress. 'Assertiveness' is not to be confused with 'aggressiveness'.

Aggressiveness is a negative attitude that does not value others and attempts to exercise power over others. Assertiveness is a positive attitude that helps you value yourself and others and to respect others while seeking respect from others in return.

> **The goal of assertiveness is to stand up for your rights without violating those of others'.**

Here are a few basic rights that we all possess but you may have forgotten (Smith, 1975):

- I have the right to express my feelings.
- I have the right to be listened to.
- I have the right to be fed up or happy.
- I have the right to be myself.
- I have the right to change my mind.
- I have the right to express my opinions.
- I have the right to say yes if I want to.
- I have the right to say no if I want to.
- I have the right to make mistakes and be responsible for them.
- I have the right to make reasonable requests from others.
- I have the right not to take responsibility for others' problems.

Which of the above rights is important to you?

. . . .

. . . .

How to be assertive

1. Look at your rights and decide what you want.
2. Say what you want to happen to resolve the situation. Be polite and keep your message short and direct, sticking to your statement and don't wander off the point.
3. Listen to the other person because they have rights also.
4. Settle on a practical agreement that both of you get something of what you want.

In which situations do you wish you were more assertive?

. . . .

. . . .

. . . .

. . . .

What could you do to achieve this?

. . . .

. . . .

. . . .

. . . .

If you can develop your assertiveness, this will be the first step for you to gain more confidence in yourself and will help with your self-esteem (what you believe about yourself).

Some tips on being confident and feeling better about yourself are:

■ List some of the things that you are good at and what you have achieved and are proud of

. . . .

. . . .

. . . .

. . . .

■ List some compliments people have said about you (whether you believe them or not)

. . . .

. . . .

. . . .

. . . .

Believe in yourself

▶ WHAT EFFECT WILL MY ILLNESS HAVE ON MY RELATIONSHIPS WITH MY FAMILY AND FRIENDS?

Has your illness caused you to have difficulties with your family?

. . . .

Your family can become very confused and concerned about some of your beliefs and behaviour. In the 1960s it was a popular belief that families caused schizophrenia. This idea was eventually rejected, but what is known is that a family's attitudes can affect the outcome of their relative's diagnosis. 'Family environment was a better predictor of rehospitalization than baseline ratings of clinical status, indicating the importance of family support in the community adjustment of chronic psychiatric patients' (Spiegel & Wissler, 1986: 58).

Your illness may cause you to behave in a way that confuses, upsets or worries your family. Can you describe any such behaviours?

. . . .

. . . .

. . . .

Are you able to understand why your family might be confused?

. . . .

. . . .

Your family may feel confused because of some of the positive symptoms of your illness, for example delusions or hallucinations. There may have been times when you also were confused by your experiences; so maybe you can understand how your family might be feeling.

Your illness may cause you to behave in a way that makes your family frustrated with you. Can you describe any such behaviours?

. . . .

. . . .

. . . .

Are you able to understand why your family might be frustrated?

. . . .

. . . .

Your family may feel frustrated because of the negative symptoms of your illness, for example lack of energy and motivation. They can find these symptoms particularly difficult and may become critical towards you because they don't understand how your illness affects you personally. This is due to your family having not received enough information regarding your illness.

Your illness may cause you to behave in a way that makes your family angry with you. Can you describe any such behaviours?

. . . .

. . . .

. . . .

Are you able to understand why your family might be angry?

. . . .

. . . .

Your family may be feeling stressed because they do not understand some of your symptoms, or because you refuse to take medication or continue to use illegal drugs or alcohol. These would be understandable reasons why your family may feel angry with you; this is because they are afraid and concerned for you.

Some families also find the changes in you very distressing and try to look after you like a child in an attempt to try and protect you; but this can seem to you like over involvement and again cause problems between you and your family.

But if your family is tolerant and understanding about your illness, then the likelihood of your symptoms worsening will be greatly reduced.

Many families do not know how to respond to the changes in their relatives who suffer from an illness such as schizophrenia. They need a lot of guidance and direction; so have patience with them.

As we know, all families have disagreements, but don't tackle your differences of opinion with a row. Find ways of getting on with your family. Talking is one of the best ways of working things out and for avoiding misunderstandings.

If you had problems within your family due to the changes in you because of your illness, what understanding do you have now on how your family managed to cope?

. . . .

. . . .

. . . .

. . . .

What could you do to prevent disagreements with your family?

. . . .

. . . .

. . . .

As a family, it is very important that you learn how to cope with this illness together; some families feel afraid, hurt, guilty and angry; however, this is not meant to be directed at you personally (although it may seem like it at times) but at the illness. Your family need to learn about your illness and to work with you and health professionals to help minimise any difficulties.

A nearest relative has the legal right to request a mental health assessment from an approved social worker (ASW) to look at the best treatment for you, and one of those decisions may be whether you need to be detained in hospital or not.

Has this happened to you?

. . . .

If so, how did you feel?

. . . .

. . . .

. . . .

What emotions do you think your family felt?

. . . .

. . . .

. . . .

Many families feel grief-stricken when this happens, but they would only use it as a last resort if they believed that you were too unwell to make the decision yourself or that an admission into hospital was in your best interests and also helped to protect the safety of others. Don't be angry with them: they are helping you (although you might not think it at the time).

This is why it is very important that a plan is agreed between you and your relatives regarding your advanced directive (see page 85) so that relatives can get help for you without feeling guilty or adversely affecting their relationship with you.

Working with your family regarding your relapse drill (page 87) and relapse signature (page 84–85) will help your family to know and identify your early-warning signs and for them to take some form of action, which might be either reminding you to take your medication or contacting health professionals for advice.

Again have some patience with your family and give them time to understand you and your illness, and remember that they want to help you but don't know how to; it is part of your responsibility to find ways of working together as a family.

> **The relationship with your family is an important part of your recovery: so make it a good relationship.**

Another important relationship to consider is an intimate one. Are you in a loving relationship with anyone at the moment?

. . . .

If you are, has your illness caused you to have problems within your relationship?

. . . .

Or are you having problems developing a relationship due to your illness?

. . . .

. . . .

It's very difficult meeting someone, even for those who have no illness: so how do you tell a new partner that you suffer from schizophrenia?

In the beginning, let your girlfriend/boyfriend get to know *you* first, not the illness. Be yourself, and develop a friendship to start with, and avoid getting too emotionally attached until you are sure you are similar in temperament and values; this way you can protect yourself from getting emotionally hurt if things don't work out further on down the road. This applies to all relationships, whether the people in them are suffering from schizophrenia or not.

Have you had any experience of telling a potential partner that you have schizophrenia? How did they react?

. . . .

. . . .

If you are seriously thinking of embarking on an intimate relationship, you have to be open and truthful regarding your condition. Being honest saves any problems later on.

How would you go about mentioning the subject of your illness?

. . . .

. . . .

. . . .

. . . .

. . . .

Discussing the subject of schizophrenia first is one way of finding out your potential partner's views on the subject. This way you can establish whether any myths need to be dispelled. As mentioned in Session 1, there is much ignorance regarding the general public's view of schizophrenia.

The next step would be to be upfront and honest and inform your potential partner that you suffer from schizophrenia.

How difficult or easy do you think this will be for you?

. . . .

. . . .

The risk of losing a potential partner who does not understand your illness is a possibility, but people with other illnesses also have this problem, but it is a risk you have to take. This is why it is important that you do not get too emotionally involved before you tell them. The risk of you getting hurt will be less.

Can you think of any other illnesses whose sufferers might find it equally difficult to disclose their condition to their partners?

. . . .

. . . .

. . . .

Give your potential partner some information on the subject of schizophrenia and let them know how your illness personally affects you in particular and how you cope. And if they see that you have control of your illness, they would be more likely to enter a relationship with you.

If not, then you have to understand that they have much to learn regarding schizophrenia. Also there may be other personal reasons of their own other than your illness for why they don't want an intimate relationship with you.

Can you think of reasons why intimate couples don't continue their relationship?

. . . .

. . . .

. . . .

. . . .

. . . .

. . . .

. . . .

. . . .

Don't take it personally, and remember to tell your partner about your illness before the relationship has developed into something deeper than fondness or physical attraction. Once you have fallen in love, a break-up will affect you much harder if things don't work out as you wanted them to – and a break-up is more likely if your partner believes that you haven't been honest with them (by not telling them you suffer from schizophrenia).

What you also need to consider is how controlled your illness is before embarking on a relationship. This means you will need to ask yourself the following questions:

- Am I compliant with my medication?
- Have I workable coping strategies regarding stress?
- Have I stopped using illegal drugs or alcohol?
- Do I have regular contact with health professionals?
- Do I fully understand my illness?

If the answer is no to any of these questions, do you think you are being reasonable to your partner or any potential children?

Which of the above list have you not achieved yet?

....

....

....

What are your plans to achieve the above?

....

....

....

What are the advantages of developing an intimate relationship with an in-patient in hospital or someone with a similar illness as yourself?

....

....

....

One of the advantages is feeling understood by someone with a similar illness; this is understandable.

What are the disadvantages of developing an intimate relationship with an in-patient in hospital or someone with a similar illness as yourself?

....

....

....

One of the disadvantages is that each party needs to remember that they have been admitted to hospital because they are both unwell and emotionally vulnerable.

Because of this, you may develop problems within this relationship causing you more stress, which may worsen your symptoms.

What problems have you developed, or could you develop, if you were involved in an intimate relationship with a partner who was mentally unwell and emotionally vulnerable?

. . . .

. . . .

. . . .

. . . .

. . . .

. . . .

A friendship would be a much more beneficial relationship for you; but what would be more valuable to you would be an intimate partner who has the same attitudes towards their illness (regarding not taking illegal drugs or the desire to have some control over their illness, for example) as you do.

This would be the starting point for you to have a successful and loving relationship.

What do you think makes a successful loving relationship?

. . . .

. . . .

. . . .

. . . .

. . . .

Intimate relationships are severely tested in response to symptoms of schizophrenia, but communication is the key to a committed, loving relationship which is based on shared values, openness and trust. (www.mentalhelp.net)

What would you need to be doing that would make your partner feel loved and secure?

. . . .

. . . .

. . . .

. . . .

. . . .

> **Trust and affection are the glue that holds couples together.**

What nice thing could you do for your partner that would please them?

. . . .

. . . .

. . . .

. . . .

. . . .

Doing something nice together, for example having a meal out, a walk in the park or listening to music. You must also find time to 'be there' for each other, and it is vital to maintain some fun and humour in your relationship.

Bringing up children can throw relationships into chaos mainly because you are forced to cope with the struggle and demands of the role but having children can also create positive change in most relationships. This also goes for couples who do not have any illnesses.

Session 2 discusses the risks involved of the child developing schizophrenia if either one or both parents has schizophrenia, but it needs to be mentioned, though, that children need the support of *both* parents, meaning that it is the parent who suffers from schizophrenia's responsibility to keep themselves as well as they can, including refraining from using any substances that might worsen their condition.

A sexually loving relationship allows partners to share in physical pleasure, comfort and also releases tension and helps couples to connect together. Family-planning advice needs to be sought also.

As already mentioned in Session 5, some medications might interfere with sexual functioning, although it is unusual for medication to be the one and only cause of sexual problems. Your libido (sex drive) can also be affected by your emotional or physical health (Dean, 2006).

Some antipsychotic medication has been known to interfere with sexual function but also many other medications can also cause sexual problems (Dean, 2006), such as medication to treat:

- blood pressure and cholesterol
- depression
- epilepsy
- ulcers and acid reflux
- insomnia
- nausea or vomiting
- fluid retention
- pain.

If this is a problem for you, ask your doctor to review all your medication.

For emotional issues ask for help from a counsellor.

If you take on board the issues discussed in this workbook, you will have a good start to having a happy and loving relationship; having the diagnosis of schizophrenia should not be a deterrent.

▶ End-of-session Questionnaire

What three important things have you learnt and will take away with you from Session 6 (you may need to browse through the session to jog your memory)?

1) ....
....
....
....
....
....
....
....
....
....

2) ....
....
....
....
....
....
....
....
....

3) ....
....
....
....
....
....
....
....

We are coming to the close of these sessions now and I hear a sigh of relief, but I hope that the sessions have been helpful for you in understanding your illness. Well done for sticking with it, as there must have been times when it must have been difficult for you. I hope your confidence is greater now than when you started these sessions and that you have more hope for your future.

The most important thing to take away from these sessions now is to be alert to your illness returning, **you have the skills** now because you have learnt about:

- your relapse signature
- your relapse drill
- what your triggers are
- working out a signed action plan
- identifying coping strategies you can use.

It is also important to note that despite your well-laid-out action plan, you may still relapse. If this happens, still make the plan useful by reviewing and refining it and use the extra knowledge gained to improve your skills.

All you need to do now is be aware and take action! Good luck!

Look after yourself.

Bibliography and Further Reading

Session 1

Association of the British Pharmaceutical Industry (2003) Target schizophrenia, http://www.abpi.org.uk/publications/publication_details/targetSchizophrenia-2003/section2.asp.

Birchwood, M. and Smith, J. (1996) *Understanding Psychosis: What Is Psychosis?* Northern Birmingham Mental Health Trust.

National Institute of Mental Health (2006) Schizophrenia facts and statistics, http://www.schizophrenia. com/szfacts.htm.

National Schizophrenia Fellowship (2001) *Help Is At Hand: Guidance for the General Public.* NSF/Royal College of Psychiatrists, London.

Pearsall, J. and Trumble, B. (2003) *Oxford English Reference Dictionary*, Oxford, Oxford University Press.

Session 2

Birchwood, M. and Smith, J. (1996) *Understanding Psychosis: What Is Psychosis?* Northern Birmingham Mental Health Trust.

Chapman, J. (2002) How cannabis can trigger schizophrenia. *Daily Mail* (3rd July), http://www.dailymail. co.uk/pages/live/articles/health/thehealthnews.html?in_article_id=126056&in_page_id=1797.

Doughty, S. (2006) 8 out of 10 mentally ill patients are heavy cannabis users. *Mail on Sunday* (16th October), http://www.mailonsunday.co.uk/pages/live/articles/news/news.html?in_article_id=410765&in_page_id=1770.

Leff, J. (1996) True Stories: *Edge of Madness*. London, Broadcasting Support Services.

Rethink (2006) Dual diagnosis, http://www.rethink.org/about_mental_illness/dual_diagnosis/ index.html.

Session 3

Chapman, J. (2002) 'How cannabis can trigger schizophrenia'; Daily Mail (3rd July), http://www.dailymail.co.uk/pages/live/articles/health/thehealthnews.html?in_article_id=126056&in_page_id=1797.

Marieb, E.N. (1989) *Human Anatomy and Physiology*. Redwood City, CA, The Benjamin-Cummings Publishing Company.

National Institute of Mental Health (2004) Schizophrenia gene variant linked to risk traits, http://www.nimh.nih.gov/press/prschizgene.cfm.

Schizophrenia.com (2006) Famous people and schizophrenia, http://www.schizophrenia.com/ famous.htm.

Session 4

Birchwood, M. and Smith, J. (1996) *Understanding Psychosis: What Is Psychosis?* Northern Birmingham Mental Health Trust.

Chadwick, P. (2000) Spiritual experience or religious psychosis? *Nursing Times* 96 (16): 42–43.

Chadwick, P., Birchwood, M. and Trower, P. (1996) *Cognitive Therapy for Delusions, Voices And Paranoia*. Chichester, Wiley.

Royal College of Psychiatrists (2003) Symptoms of schizophrenia, http://www.rcpsych.ac.uk/ mentalhealthinformation/mentalhealthproblems/schizophrenia/schizophrenia/ symptomsofschizophrenia.aspx.

Stuttaford, T. and Sharma, T. (1999) *In Your Right Mind*. London, Faber and Faber.

Session 5

Goff D.C., Henderson, D.C., Amico, E. (1992) Cigarette smoking in schizophrenia: relationship to psychopathology and medication side effects, *American Journal of Psychiatry* 149 (9): 1189, http://ajp.psychiatryonline.org/cgi/content/abstract/149/9/1189.

Lewis, S.W., Davies, L. Jones, P.B. *et al.* (2006) Randomised controlled trials of conventional antipsychotic versus new atypical drugs, and new atypical drugs versus clozapine, in people with schizophrenia responding poorly to, or intolerant of, current drug treatment, http://www.hta.ac.uk/execsumm/summ1017.htm.

Mind (2004) Making sense of antipsychotics, http://www.mind.org.uk/Information/Booklets/ Making+sense/antip.htm.

Mind (2006) The Mental Health Act 1983: an outline guide, http://www.mind.org.uk/Information/ Legal/OGMHA.htm.

National Alliance for the Mentally Ill (2003) NAMI sees cure for schizophrenia as possible in 10 years, http://www.schizophrenia.com/New/sz.news.120103.htm#nami.

Taylor, D., Paton C. and Kerwin, R. (2005) *The Maudsley 2005–2006: Prescribing Guidelines* (8th edition). Abingdon, Taylor and Francis.

Winston, A.P., Hardwick, E., Jaberi, N. (2005) Neuropsychiatric effects of caffeine, *Advances in Psychiatric Treatment* 11: 432–39, http://apt.rcpsych.org/cgi/content/full/11/6/432.

Session 6

Birchwood, M. Spencer, E. and McGovern, D. (2000) Schizophrenia: early warning signs. *Advances in Psychiatric Treatment* 6 (2): 93–101, http://apt.rcpsych.org/cgi/content/full/6/2/93.

Chadwick, P., Birchwood, M. and Trower, P. (1996) *Cognitive Therapy for Delusions, Voices And Paranoia*. Chichester, Wiley.

Dean, J. (2006) Medication disrupting your sex life, http://www.netdoctor.co.uk/menshealth/feature/medicinessex.htm.

http://mentalhelp.net/poc/view_doc.php?type=doc&id=4397&cn=289

Smith, J. (2005) *Self-management Training Manual*. Community First in Herefordshire and Worcestershire Mental Health Partnership NHS Trust, WCC Social Service Department and the Mental Health Link Project.

Smith, M.J. (1975) *When I Say No, I Feel Guilty*, London, Bantam, http://www.bbc.co.uk/dna/h2g2/ A2998551.

Spiegel, D. and Wissler, T. (1986) Family environment as a predictor of psychiatric rehospitalization. *American Journal of Psychiatry* 143 (1): 56–60.

Further resources

For more information on assertiveness training, visit:

'Assertiveness communication' at http://www.uiowa.edu/~ucs/asertcom.html.

To help readers learn more about 'voices':

The Voice Inside: A Practical Guide to Coping with Hearing Voices (1995) by Paul Baker; Handsell Publications, Manchester.

Working with Voices: Victim to Victor (1997) by Ron Coleman and Mike Smith; Handsell Publications, Kingsteignton.

For more information on drug misuse and schizophrenia, visit the following websites from Schizophrenia.com:

http://www.schizophrenia.com/sznews/archives/003851.html
http://www.schizophrenia.com/prevention/streetdrugs.html#video

Some useful addresses and telephone numbers

Hearing Voices Network

79 Lever Street
Manchester
M1 1FL
(0845) 122 8641
www.hearing-voices.org

Rethink (formerly the National Schizophrenia Fellowship)

28 Castle Street
Kingston upon Thames
Surrey
KT1 1BR
(020) 8974 6814
www.rethink.org

Samaritans

The Upper Mill
Kingston Road
Ewell
Surrey KT17 2AF
(08457) 90 90 90
www.samaritans.org

Mind

15–19 Broadway
London
E15 4BO
(020) 8519 2122
contact@mind.org.uk

British Association for Behavioural & Cognitive Psychotherapists

The Globe Centre
PO Box 9
Accrington
Lancashire
BB5 0XB
(01254) 875 277

Index